Sushi Cookbook

80+ Easy Recipes to Make Sushi at Home

Haru Okamoto

Table of Contents

Introduction

Today sushi is not just Japanese food; it's popular and fashionable all around the world. Many sushi recipes are works of art and are wonderfully centered on multicultural trends.

Sushi chefs create standard Japanese sushi. Technically, they are called craftsmen in Japan, not cooks, and the sushi they create is considered to be an essential art. The explanation for using this terminology is that being a sushi chef normally takes three to five years, and to do so requires specific techniques and a lot of patience to maintain the old practices. In the first year, chefs in college are unable to learn how to make sushi but must learn how to disinfect a restaurant, deliver, cook rice, and service clients. They will begin learning to cook sushi in earnest over the first year. Without looking every time they create nigiri sushi, a professional sushi chef will catch precisely the same weight and the same volume of rice grains, and the rice is not crushed but retains its form fully. It is this sheer perfection in craftsmanship that encourages

Japanese people to go out to cafes rather than making sushi at home.

High-quality sushi is delicious, but it can be rather pricey. So nowadays, many people are attempting to create their own sushi, including in Japan. Homemade sushi is meant to be tasty, simple to produce, and stunning. For individuals to create at home, there are many global, nontraditional, awe-inspiring sushi recipes.

My mother and my grandmother also created traditional sushi rolls and inari sushi (a common Japanese rice ball) when I was a boy. It was the greatest sushi I've ever had. The seasoned rice tasted distinct, even though the toppings are the same as conventional recipes. This is one of the benefits of handmade sushi-adjusting the seasoning and incorporating some ingredients as fillings according to personal preference. I heard a lot from my mother and grandmother about food, who made me enjoy the beauty of producing sushi. I'm here to teach you how and that it isn't hard to make sushi. You, too, should do it.

I kept the recipes clear and used ingredients in this book that are quick to locate and accessible in the United

States. Seafood, beef, vegetarian, and vegan sushi dishes are eligible. As an extra bonus, if you use gluten-free soy sauce most sushi is gluten-free. There are also several recipes in this book to help you cook good-looking sushi. You will need a bit of practice, but you will be able to make your own sushi quickly with this cookbook. Only follow the recipes, and you can enjoy your favorite sushi without rushing out to a sushi restaurant whenever you want.

Chapter 1: Starting your sushi journey

It is not complicated at all to make homemade sushi and this eBook is your guide. It includes all the simple stuff you need to learn about sushi, how to cook it, the tools you need, the materials, the manners, the style of serving, and helpful tips. With good faith effort and a focus on fun, this book will completely train you to make sushi!

1.1 The History of Sushi

People fermented fresh fish with salt and rice around 1,300 years ago to protect it. This was the sushi starting. The rice was used as an ingredient for fermentation, though, and only the fish was consumed. Even today, this style is embodied in Shiga prefecture's famed regional sushi cuisine, named funazushi.

Sushi, as we know it today, during the Edo period, nigiri sushi and sushi rolls originated around 400 years ago. There were fancy sushi restaurants and sushi stalls at the time. The sushi from the stand was consumed like fast food by busy citizens. The disparity is the scale of the present nigiri and Edo-era nigiri. The Edo-era nigiri, which is bite-size, was 1.5 times thicker than the present nigiri.

While sushi was a very common meal, due to a scarcity of food, sushi restaurants were closed after World War II by food regulators. Some restaurants introduced improvements to their strategy to get around this and allowed their customers to carry their own rice, which was then combined with sushi from the restaurant as Japan saw accelerated economic development and prosperity, food policy policies modified again, enabling sushi service in restaurants. For the sushi business, the year 1958 was pivotal: it was the first year clients could go to a sushi bar and buy prepared sushi from a conveyor belt. Fancy sushi restaurants are still visited these days; nevertheless, sushi bars are the most common.

In 1887, in San Francisco, a Japanese immigrant founded the first sushi restaurant in the United States. During World War II, though all sushi restaurants operated by Japanese citizens were closed due to Japanese Americans being interned. The restaurants steadily returned after the war, and the sushi boom progressively spread from the 1970s onwards. In addition to the rise in popularity of sushi restaurants in the United States, US-based Japanese sushi chefs have developed many non-traditional sushi recipes to conform to the abundance of ingredients and to suit American tastes. For one, for Americans, uramaki, a sushi roll with rice on the outside, was developed because many Americans did not like the sensation of consuming nori, edible seaweed.

1.2 Tools

Beginners may not require a lot of supplies, although there are a few useful materials. To help you prioritize, below are my suggestions for must-haves and nice to have.

Must-Haves

MAKISU (SUSHI-ROLLING MAT) – A sushi-rolling mat is a vital tool for visually spectacular sushi development. The mats are constructed of bamboo, rubber, or acrylic. Due to its versatility, I suggest a bamboo pad, which allows it much simpler to uniformly roll 7-to-8-inch-long sushi rolls. As it has antibacterial properties and prevents odors, bamboo is often extremely sanitary. It requires great attention, though. To get rid of any debris as well as the bamboo odor before the first usage, it is essential to boil the pad. Whenever you see rice or other sushi products trapped between the bamboo poles, wash immediately with a clean wet kitchen towel since it is difficult to wash after the debris dries (you can avoid this problem by placing a piece of parchment paper or some plastic wrap on the bamboo mat). Handwash your makisu with water (dish soap is not recommended) and dry very well without intense sunlight in a shady place. I'm not a fan of silicone or acrylic mats at all. Since the silicone mats are too soft and the plastic mats are too rigid, they are not as easy to roll.

SHAMOJI (RICE PADDLE) – I strongly recommend getting a self-standing, plastic rice paddle with a gritty surface that is non-stick since it has the perfect form for rice blending and scooping. It is quick to use this sort of paddle and helps keep the kitchen tidy. It is also the one method that I can't find any alternatives for. There are wooden paddles of rice, so it's so easy for the rice to adhere to, which is stressful because they can't go through the dishwasher.

Nice to Have

RICE COOKER – This is a helpful method to have, but not necessary because I'm going to show you how to cook rice in a skillet. It makes things simpler and more effective if you have a rice cooker.

CUTTING BOARDS – Frequent cutting includes sushi making. It's better to use separate plates for raw seafood, fruits, fried foods, and meats for protection. For general usage of vegetables and cooked food and dishwasher-safe boards for seafood and beef, I propose wooden cutting boards. As they are knife-friendly, I prefer wooden boards. They are often easy on the hand since the cutting vibration is absorbed by the paper. For long periods, when you use boards made of hard materials such as glass, you expose your hand to direct shocks any time you break through the board with the knife, and this leaves your hand tired. The trick to a wooden board is to wash regularly and sanitize after cutting fish or meat roughly once a week and any time with boiling water.

SUSHI-OKE, HANGIRI, OR HANDAI (RICE-MIXING TUB) – This is a wood-based shallow tub used to combine steamed rice and sushi vinegar. For cooling sushi rice down, it has a perfect design, and it looks good at a party or in photographs. Please bear in mind that it is a little challenging to handle this tool. For this, you should certainly substitute a wide bowl or a high-rimmed baking sheet.

THE KNIFE

There are so many types of knives that deciding which one to purchase is often overwhelming. You might ask them for a suggestion if there's a cutler near you. Before making a pick, make sure to keep the knives in your grip to evaluate their heaviness and comfort. If you don't have a cutler nearby, don't worry; I'll clarify how to pick a decent sushi knife.

How to Choose the Right Knife

You need a sharp knife that cuts when pulling the knife in one cut into you for slicing seafood and cutting sushi rolls smoothly. When you carve, a blunt knife crushes the ingredients. Look for a yanagiba knife or a sashimi knife that has a broad, thin tip, whether you choose to purchase a decent sushi knife. For these blades, three styles of blade materials exist carbon steel, stainless steel, and ceramic. In typical Japanese blades, carbon steel is the material and is the sharpest, but it can rust quickly. It is simple to handle with stainless steel and ceramic blades, but they are not as effective as carbon steel. Yanagiba knives often have a single tip, but you can aim for a double-bevel range if you are left-handed or inquire about testing it before purchasing it. Choosing a blade that is 8 to 10 inches long and shorter than the cutting board is safer. For cutting sashimi, I prefer using a stainless steel yanagiba knife because it slices smoothly, is simple to manage, and typically does not rust. Bear in mind that these knives are meant for cutting fresh seafood, but do not use them for cutting frozen fish, bones of fish, or other rough ingredients. It is possible to simply sever the tip of the knife.

1.3 Fresh Ingredients

The main reason is that it includes fresh seafood and vegetables is one of the explanations that sushi is safe. I mention the important fresh sushi ingredients here, and I'm showing you how to pick healthy seafood.

SEAFOOD

SMOKED SALMON – Smoked salmon brings great, rich flavor to your sushi dishes. Store-bought smoked salmon is ready to use and has a longer usage life than fresh salmon when stored in the refrigerator. It is a handy and safe food.

TUNA (MAGURO) – Served raw in sashimi and sushi dishes. There are many kinds of tuna used for sushi, such as bluefin, bigeye, yellowfin, and albacore. You can buy any kind of tuna. Choose sashimi-grade meat that has a bright red color and an even grain. Avoid dark or discolored tuna. This means the tuna is old.

SHRIMP (EBI) – When using for nigiri sushi and as a topping on chirashi sushi, buy medium-size, tail-on, un-deveined shrimp. Cooking sushi shrimp requires a little technique.

The details and some tips can be found in the recipes in this book that use boiled shrimp.

SEARED BONITO (KATSUO-NO-TATAKI) – Bonito fillet is grilled briefly before being sliced and served with ponzu sauce.

YELLOWTAIL (HAMACHI) – Hamachi is a very popular fish for sashimi and nigiri in Japan. It has a light taste and tender texture. Choose translucent meat with red muscle.

SALMON – Salmon has healthy fat and it tastes very mild. It is a popular ingredient for making sashimi and sushi dishes. Be sure to choose sashimi-grade frozen salmon that is properly treated because salmon can have anisakis (a parasite). If you really care about parasitic insects, choose only farm-raised salmon. Studies show that farm-raised fish may have fewer parasitic insects than wild-caught fish. This is true not only for salmon but also for other ocean fish. It is also important to check the fish visually when you cut. Choose salmon that has clear strings (connective tissue) if you can see them.

SALMON ROE (IKURA) – Great for gunkanmaki and sometimes to eat on its own. The roe pops in the mouth and then brings a very mild yet rich, delicious taste. You may find glass jars of salmon roe at grocery stores or online seafood shops.

SCALLOP (HOTATE) – Served as a sashimi dish and in nigiri sushi. It has a sweet taste and a very soft texture. Try eating it with natural sea salt. The flavor is more pronounced than when eating it with soy sauce. Most store-bought sashimi-grade scallops are frozen. If you find fresh scallops, choose meaty, thick ones. Do not rinse scallops with water because this makes them taste bland.

CRABMEAT (KANI) – When the meat is a lump, it is great for making gunkanmaki. When the meat is well-shaped, like crab legs, it is good for making nigiri sushi and sushi rolls. Also, canned crabmeat is very handy and delicious.

NEGITORO – Minced sashimi tuna garnished with chopped scallion. It is served as a sushi roll and in gunkanmaki. It has a great, fluffy texture.

Picking the Right Fish

CHOOSE THE RIGHT FISHMONGER – A significant guide for selecting a fishmonger is feedback. Freshness, odor, how the fish are displayed (on ice), and the shop's cleanliness are crucial to having fish of the right size. Ask and check web ratings from your friends and neighbors. There are also several online seafood shops that can be helpful for individuals residing in landlocked areas.

VISUAL CHECK – Check that the meat is glossy, clean, tight, solid, and brightly colored when purchasing a sashimi-grade fish fillet. Check the fillet and pick one that has fewer deicing oil, which you'll see in the case or in the box as a murky, slightly thick substance around the fish. If there is a lot of deicing fluid in the fillet, that means it might have been easily thawed, making the fish taste bland and smell foul.

PRODUCE AND OTHER FRESH ITEMS

CUCUMBER – A useful ingredient for sushi rolls and beautiful addition to gunkanmaki. Also, cut and carved cucumber in decorative shapes, such as flowers, is sometimes used as a garnish for sashimi dishes.

EGG – An essential ingredient for traditional Japanese sushi dishes.

LEAF LETTUCE – There is a traditional "salad sushi roll" with lettuce, canned tuna, imitation crab, mayonnaise, and sometimes sweet corn kernels with nori and sushi rice. Also, lettuce sometimes becomes a substitute for nori for hand-roll sushi (temaki).

AVOCADO – This is an extremely popular ingredient that was not a traditional ingredient for sushi in Japan. About 50 years ago, sushi restaurants started serving avocado sushi, and now the Japanese love it very much.

IMITATION CRABMEAT – Very handy ingredient made with fish meat paste and good in many kinds of sushi dishes.

CREAM CHEESE – Used for sushi rolls. It goes really well with salmon and shrimp.

SWEET ONION – Marinated sweet onion is used as a garnish for salmon nigiri sushi and is eaten on its own as a side dish.

CORN – Versatile ingredient used for many kinds of sushi dishes. It is one of the popular sushi ingredients for kids in Japan.

SHIITAKE MUSHROOMS AND SPINACH

Both ingredients are essentials for traditional sushi rolls. They are traditionally cooked with a sweet-savory dashi sauce.

ASPARAGUS – Boiled or fried asparagus is a great ingredient for sushi rolls and can also be a garnish for creative sushi rolls.

CARROT AND RADISH – Both are used as a garnish for sushi dishes. As with cucumber, cut and carved carrots and radishes in decorative shapes, such as flowers, are sometimes used as a garnish for sashimi dishes.

MEATS – Sometimes meat, such as chicken, beef, bacon, or ham, is used for homemade sushi dishes. This practice is in its infancy in sushi restaurants in Japan, with roast beef and roast duck nigiri sushi being very popular.

DAIKON RADISH – Important garnish for sashimi dishes. It has antibacterial effects and reduces the chance of contracting food poisoning. Slice into very thin strips and place sashimi on the daikon radish to serve.

SHISO (PERILLA/JAPANESE BASIL) – A Japanese herb that grows naturally in Japan. It is used as a garnish for sashimi dishes. As with daikon radish, it has antibacterial effects and reduces the risk of food poisoning. Substitute basil leaf or parsley, which has microbicidal properties.

Pantry Ingredients

I'm going to show you some ingredients that you can store in your pantry here. Few convenient dried and canned ingredients are also available that you can swap for fresh ingredients. In Asian markets or on Amazon, you will get any of these.

SUSHI NORI – This type of dried seaweed usually comes in 7-by-8-inch sheets. There are two sides—one is shiny, and the other is slightly rough—and traditionally, sushi rice is placed on the rough side. Once the package is opened, put the nori in a zip-top bag and keep it in the refrigerator.

SHORT-GRAIN WHITE RICE (SUSHI RICE) – Stock in the pantry and, once it is opened, put the rice with its bag in a zip-top bag and keep it in the refrigerator.

DRIED KELP (DASHI KOMBU) – Cooking sushi rice with dried kelp adds a richer, umami flavor to the rice.

SOY SAUCE – Generally, people say sashimi-grade fish goes well with tamari soy sauce. There are about 10,000 kinds of soy sauce in Japan alone, so it can be good to find your favorite soy sauce for your sushi. Once it's opened, keep it in the refrigerator unless otherwise instructed.

WASABI PASTE/WASABI POWDER – For the paste type of wasabi, once it's opened, keep it in the refrigerator. For the powder type, close the lid tightly and keep it in the pantry.

ROASTED SESAME SEEDS – Used to garnish the outside of uramaki sushi rolls and sometimes mixed in sushi rice.

CANNED SEASONED FRIED BEAN CURD – This makes cooking inari sushi much easier, and it is definitely a time-saver.

PICKLED SUSHI GINGER (GARI) – If fresh young ginger, the central ingredient of homemade pickled sushi ginger, cannot be found, store-bought pickled ginger is very useful. Once it's opened, keep it in the refrigerator.

DASHI STOCK POWDER – Used for simmering sushi vegetables and soups. Bonito dashi powder, which is the most common, is useful. If you would like vegetable stock, choose kombu dashi powder.

WAKAME – Used for soup, in a salad, and as a garnish for sashimi dishes. Sushi nori, wakame, and kelp are different kinds of seaweed. Wakame is thin, not gooey, easy to eat, and high in minerals.

1.4 The style of Eating Sushi

In Japanese food culture, there are multiple etiquette rules, not only for consuming sushi but even for eating other items and also at home at the dining table. Some of these customs are excessive and obsolete. As times have changed, things have begun getting more casual. For instance, eating nigiri sushi with your hands was originally considered polite, but today it is considered polite to either use chopsticks or eat by hand. Here, I mention several simple etiquette guidelines for eating at a Japanese sushi restaurant.

- You may consume sushi with either chopstick or hands directly into your mouth. In Japanese restaurants, a wet towel is served.
- Start with a moderate, light-tasting fish, and then moving to increasingly fattier fish is preferable. This is so you can appreciate tasting several kinds of seafood.
- Tilt the portion slightly to the side when you consume nigiri sushi and dip the edge of the fish in a tiny amount of soy sauce so that the rice does not

absorb much and you can appreciate the seafood's natural, new flavor. Do not cut the nigiri sushi seafood. Instead, dunk it in the soy sauce and place it on the rice again.

- Eat sushi from nigiri with one bite. Do not bite the nigiri halfway.
- Dip a sushi roll's edge in soy sauce. Sushi rolls are eaten on the hand in Japan with soy sauce and are not drizzled with mayonnaise or hot sauce.
- Dip the fish in soy sauce when you consume chirashi sushi, place it back on the rice, and then eat it all together.
- Put a little amount of wasabi on the sashimi and dunk it in soy sauce while you consume sashimi with wasabi. In the soy sauce, do not dissolve the wasabi.
- Feel free to notify the sushi chef if you do not like wasabi. Sushi chefs usually placed wasabi in most nigiri sushi and in thin sushi rolls between rice and seafood.

- Generally, people consume sashimi as an appetizer in a Japanese sushi restaurant and eat nigiri as the main course. The chefs tend to believe you've completed your meal if you order sushi rolls and a soup after that.

1.5 The Art of Sushi Serving

It is said that we assess a meal utilizing the five senses in Japanese cuisine: touch, taste, vision, scent, and sound. Visual beauty is deeply associated with taste. People seem to believe it is tastier when a meal has a lovely final appearance. However, this doesn't mean that we have to overly decorate plates. Usually, Japanese sushi is prepared easily and beautifully. The world thoroughly reflects the real natural elegance of the ingredients in sushi.

- For individuals that may drink sushi by hand, plan any wet towels individually.
- Sushi with some pickled ginger is still eaten.

- Serve with thin, shallow plates that can be packed with soy sauce, any sushi that does not have a drizzled sauce.
- Shiso (substitute basil leaves or parsley), thinly sliced daikon radish, or some decoratively cut and decorated vegetables, such as cucumber, radish, and carrot, are preferably eaten with sashimi.
- There can still be similar sizes and shapes for the same sort of sushi. Nigiri sushi, for instance, can still have the same rice size and form. Sushi rolls can have pretty circles or squares in their form.
- Garnish with some almonds, crispy fried onions, or tempura flour pieces for imaginative sushi rolls, and drizzle some sauce over the sushi rolls.

Chapter 2: Preparing your ingredients

This chapter will show you the practical measures for sushi preparation, such as preparing sushi rice, avoiding mistakes, and how to cook fish, herbs, and other items. It is important to note that there are just a few simple rules that you need to know to prepare sushi if you find all the knowledge daunting. You will have a number of choices once you grasp these simple principles since sushi production is flexible.

Rice

Sushi is historically a term for dishes that mix certain fresh foods, such as sashimi fish and/or vegetables, with vinegared rice. You can use short-grain white rice from Japan (sometimes referred to as sushi rice and sometimes accessible at your local supermarket) to make healthy sushi rice. Be sure to weigh the rice and water accurately.

There are two variations between cooking sushi rice and cooking standard rice. The soaking time for the sushi rice is shorter as you cook it in a deep bath. You can cook sushi rice with a little less water (approximately 1 tablespoon less) when you use a rice cooker than when you cook standard white rice since the rice cooker requires soaking time in the cooking phase. This is vital because, during mixing and forming, you don't want the rice to get too mushy. Second, to give a great umami taste to the rice, you can cook sushi rice with dried kelp.

2.1 Sushi Rice

GLUTEN-FREE, NUT-FREE, VEGETARIAN, VEGAN

I'm here to teach you how to make a sushi rice dish. The taste of sushi rice varies on the basis of the rice and vinegar mixture. In this recipe, you will learn how to produce a great vinegar mixture and how to blend the ingredients to make delicious sushi rice! The volume of sugar will, however, be increased or decreased in the mixture if you wish.

Yield: 4 cups (4 big rolls or 8 thin rolls or 48 pieces nigiri sushi)

Prep time: 25 minutes

Cook time: 25 minutes

Ingredients:

- 1½ cups short-grain white rice
- 1⅔ cups water
- Tablespoons rice vinegar
- 5 teaspoons sugar
- Teaspoons salt
- 1 (4-by-4-inch) piece dried kelp (dashi kombu)

Directions:

1. In a fine-mesh strainer set atop a bowl, rinse the rice under cool running water while stirring it with your hand. Drain the rice as soon as the water in the bowl turns a murky white color. Repeat until the water in the bowl is clear.

2. In a medium bowl, combine the rice and water and let soak for 15 minutes at room temperature.

3. In a small bowl, mix the rice vinegar, sugar, and salt. Set aside.

4. Pour the rice and water into a deep saucepan and add the kelp. Cover the pan and bring the mixture to a boil over high heat. Turn the heat to low and cook for 10 minutes. When there is no water left in the pan, turn off the heat, put a kitchen towel under the lid, and steam the rice for 10 minutes.

5. Remove the kelp and discard. Transfer the rice to a large mixing bowl. Add the vinegar mixture to the bowl. Using a rice paddle, fold gently to combine and coat each grain of rice with the mixture

(it is like mixing whipped egg whites into cake batter). Cover with a damp, clean cloth and allow to cool to room temperature before using the rice to make sushi.

COOKING TIP: Check the inside of the pan before throwing a kitchen towel over the rice. Put the lid back on if there is already water visible in the pan and cook for 2 more minutes, then check again.

STORAGE TIP: Move the sushi rice to a bag or glass jar in the fridge. Hold and use in the freezer within 3 weeks. Microwave the rice for 2 to 3 minutes on a microwave-safe dish, sealed, to thaw it. Move the sushi rice to a clean container, cover it, and refrigerate it for preservation in the freezer—usage within a half-day span.

HOW TO AVOID MISSHAPEN SUSHI ROLLS

When preparing sushi rolls, typical issue sushi beginners face is that the sushi nori sheet cracks, don't seal, or falls apart. Here are some fantastic answers to these problems:

- Spread the sushi rice appropriately on the nori mat. I propose spreading 1 cup of sushi rice over a whole sheet of nori (or 1/2 cup of sushi rice over a half sheet of nori). Depending upon the recipe, this number can fluctuate a bit. Spreading the rice equally requires a bit of preparation. The roll would not close or be too loose whether there is too much or too little rice. For beginners, however, I strongly suggest that you steadily scatter the rice on the nori sheet until you can't see the nori between the rice grains.

- Pick the right loading quantity and do not overfill. Too much filling induces splitting or opening of sushi rolls. Basically, begin with the filling in a close pile on the rice for a thin roll. The height of the filling pile may be less than a quarter of the thickness of the short side of the sheet of nori.
- Firmly roll. Although when the volume of rice and filling is sufficient, the rolls will not stay together if you roll loosely.
- Create loads of salmon rolls. Training adds to mastering.

FOOD SAFETY: Since sushi involves raw fish and vegetables, washing your hands regularly and utilizing multiple cutting boards for each form of ingredient is quite necessary (fish, shellfish, vegetables).

2.2 Preparing Seafood

To make a perfect final show, here are useful tips about how to thaw and cut seafood. The exact cutting processes mentioned here are not completely mandatory, but when you obey these instructions, you can have a lot simpler time making sushi.

SASHIMI-GRADE TUNA AND SALMON

1. To thaw, place unpackaged frozen fillets on a plate, cover, and refrigerate for about 10 hours.

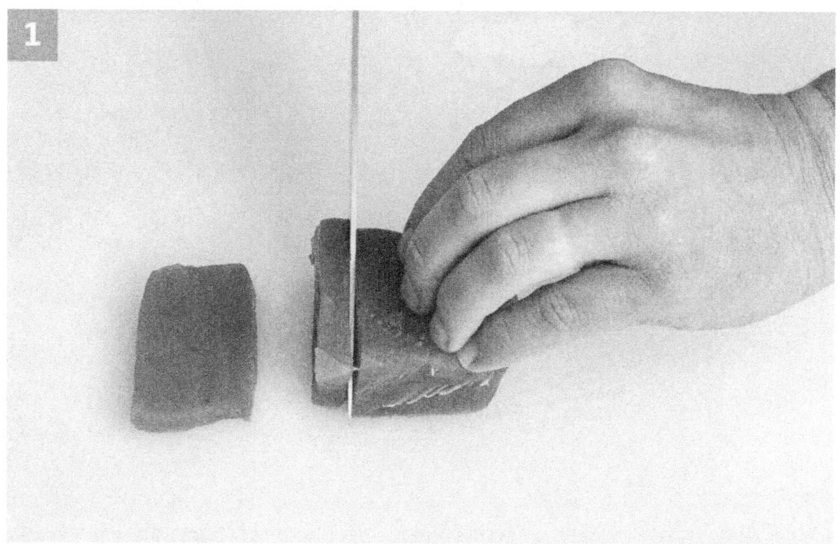

2. To remove fishy odor, wash the fillets quickly under running water and gently pat dry with paper towels.

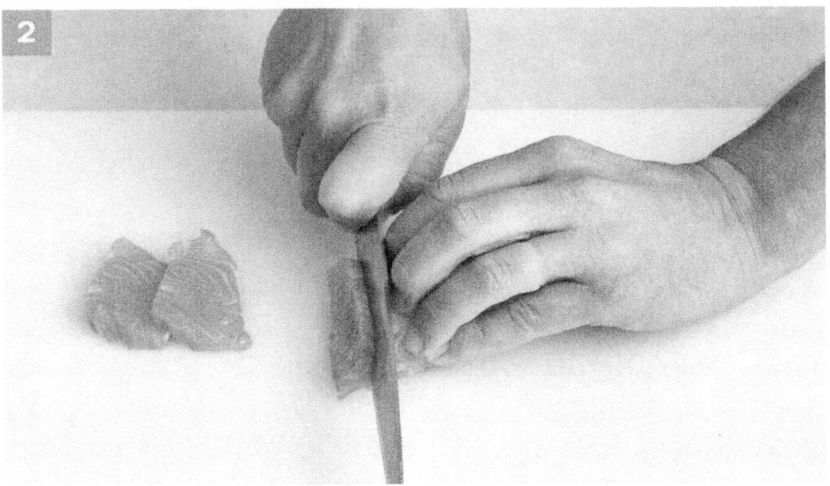

3. Cut at a right angle to the grain. For sashimi dishes, slice into approximately 1-by-2-inch pieces that are ⅓ inch thick (1). For nigiri sushi, slice in approximately 1-by-2-inch pieces that are ¼ inch thick (2). For sushi rolls, cut the fish into ½-inch-thick and 2½-inch-long sticks (3). When cutting fish for all types of sushi, carefully pull the knife toward you in one motion, so the fillet doesn't tear.

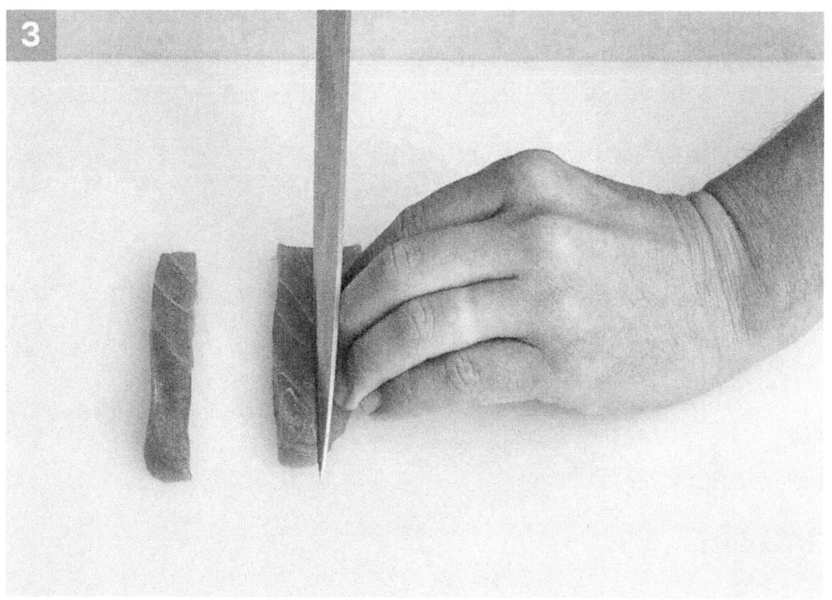

SHRIMP

1. If the shrimp are frozen, soak in salt water (1 tablespoon salt per 2 cups water) and keep in the refrigerator for 1 to 2 hours to thaw.

2. In a bowl, place the thawed shrimp (regardless of whether the shell is on or off) and sprinkle with baking soda (2 tablespoons baking soda per pound). Toss to coat for 1 minute and rinse well with water. Lay the shrimp on paper towels and use more paper towels to blot.

3. Cut the tip of the tail off (if it is tail-on) and scrape off the water on the trail with a knife. This helps remove the fishy smell and avoid oil splatters when it is fried.

4. For nigiri sushi, use shell-on, tail-on, un-deveined medium-size shrimp. For sushi rolls, use deveined medium or large shrimp. If you prefer that the tail stick out from your sushi roll for the final presentation, choose tail-on shrimp.

SCALLOPS

1. To thaw, place unpackaged frozen scallops on a plate, cover, and keep in the refrigerator for 4 to 5 hours.

2. Pat the thawed scallops dry with a paper towel. Do not rinse with water because scallops can become bland easily.

3. For sashimi dishes, halve the scallops horizontally. For nigiri sushi, make an incision from the side and butterfly.

SALMON ROE

Store-bought jarred salmon roe basically does not require preparation. But taste it before serving. If you find the taste is too salty, you can soak the roe in saltwater (1 teaspoon salt per 1 cup water) for about 30 minutes. Drain and gently pat dry with a paper towel.

2.3 Preparing Vegetables and Other Common Items

AVOCADO

For sushi rolls, cut into quarters lengthwise, remove the pit, peel, and slice lengthwise. For use as a topping, cut in half lengthwise and remove the pit. Using the knife tip, score the avocado flesh without piercing the skin and scoop it out with a spoon.

CUCUMBER

Use Persian cucumber (baby cucumber) that has low moisture, so the sushi roll doesn't become soggy. For sushi rolls, halve lengthwise, then halve lengthwise again to make sticks. To use cucumber to cover a sushi roll as a topping, slice lengthwise with a peeler or slicer. For garnishing sashimi dishes, slice diagonally or use a small cookie cutter to make decorative shapes.

IMITATION CRABMEAT

For sushi rolls, halve lengthwise if the imitation crabmeat is leg-style. When the imitation crabmeat is flaked, cut into ½-inch pieces.

LEAF LETTUCE

Wash each leaf and pat dry with a paper towel. For thin sushi rolls, halve lengthwise. For big rolls, if the leaf is shorter than the sushi nori, use without cutting. For garnishing sashimi dishes, tear into palm-sized pieces and lay some sashimi on the lettuce.

SUSHI NORI

Place the shiny nori side down and put sushi rice on the rough side of the nori. For thick (big) sushi rolls, use a whole sheet (about 7 by 8 inches). For thin rolls, halve the sheet on the long side. For gunkanmaki, cut the long side of the sheet into six equal lengths. For hand-rolled sushi, cut the sheet into quarters, so each piece of nori is approximately square.

DAIKON RADISH

For garnishing sashimi dishes, shred thinly. Traditionally, daikon should be prepared like a zucchini noodle. The surface of a ½-inch-thick columnar daikon radish should be spirally stripped toward the center (this is called katsuramuki), then the daikon sheet should be cut, so it looks like a noodle. Lay some sashimi on the shredded daikon.

Chapter 3: Sashimi, Nigiri, and Other Sushi Dishes

3.1 Sashimi

Auspicious Sashimi

GLUTEN-FREE, NUT-FREE, PESCATARIAN

This is a scallop and salmon roe sashimi dish eaten without soy sauce. Natural sea salt brings out the flavor of the fresh scallop. To eat, dredge the scallop in a very small amount of salt. To serve salmon roe as a sashimi dish, place it on a small, deep plate, like a sake cup. You can eat the roe with chopsticks or a small spoon.

Yield: 4 pieces

Prep time: 10 minutes

Cook time: 8 minutes

Ingredients:

- 1 green leaf lettuce leaf, torn into 4 pieces
- 4 sashimi-grade scallops, halved horizontally
- 1 teaspoon natural sea salt
- 4 tablespoons salmon roe Wasabi

Direc

tions:

1. Line a serving plate with lettuce, put 2 slices of scallop on each piece of lettuce, and place the salt on the corner of the plate.

2. Place 1 tablespoon of salmon roe on a deep, small plate and put a dash of wasabi on top. Repeat for three more plates with the remaining salmon roe and wasabi.

SUBSTITUTION TIP: If you can find Japanese shiso (perilla), substitute it for the green leaf lettuce.

Assorted Sashimi

GLUTEN-FREE, NUT-FREE, PESCATARIAN

There is tuna, salmon, and seared bonito in this signature sashimi dish. The food is eaten with wasabi and a little dish of soy sauce all over Japan. Each fillet is 1⁄2 pound in this recipe and makes around 4 servings. Sometimes, it is used as a side dish. You can always see people eating this easy and delicious dish if you go to a sushi restaurant or izakaya (dining bar) in Japan.

Yield: 8 pieces

Prep time: 10 minutes

Cook time: 5 minutes

Ingredients:

- Green leaf lettuce leaf, torn
- ¼ small daikon radish, shredded
- ½ pound sashimi-grade tuna, sliced
- 2 teaspoon wasabis
- ½ pound seared bonito, sliced into ⅓-inch-wide pieces
- Soy sauce (gluten-free if necessary)

- ½ pound sashimi-grade salmon, sliced

Directions:

1. Line a serving plate with the daikon, arrange the lettuce on the daikon, and make the wasabi into a mound on the corner.
2. Place the sliced tuna, salmon, and bonito on the lettuce.
3. Serve with a small, shallow dish of soy sauce for each person.

SUBSTITUTION TIP: If you can find Japanese shiso (perilla), substitute it for green leaf lettuce.

3.2 Nigiri sushi

Maguro (Tuna) Nigiri

GLUTEN-FREE, NUT-FREE, PESCATARIAN

Bright-red, fresh maguro is tantalizing and has a light taste, so it is a great nigiri starter. Nonfat maguro (which is not toro) is very healthy. It is low in calories (3 slices of maguro have about 40 kcal) and high in protein, vitamin B, and vitamin D. The prep time is 20 minutes, but it may become shorter once you get used to making the proper shape with the nigiri sushi rice.

Yield: 10 to 12 pieces

Prep time: 20 minutes

Cook time: 10 minutes

Ingredients:

- 2 cups Sushi Rice
- Wasabi
- ½ pound sashimi-grade tuna, sliced
- 2 tablespoons Pickled Sushi Ginger
- Soy sauce (gluten-free if necessary)

Directions:

1. Scoop 1 heaping tablespoon of sushi rice on your wet hand and make it into a flat football shape.

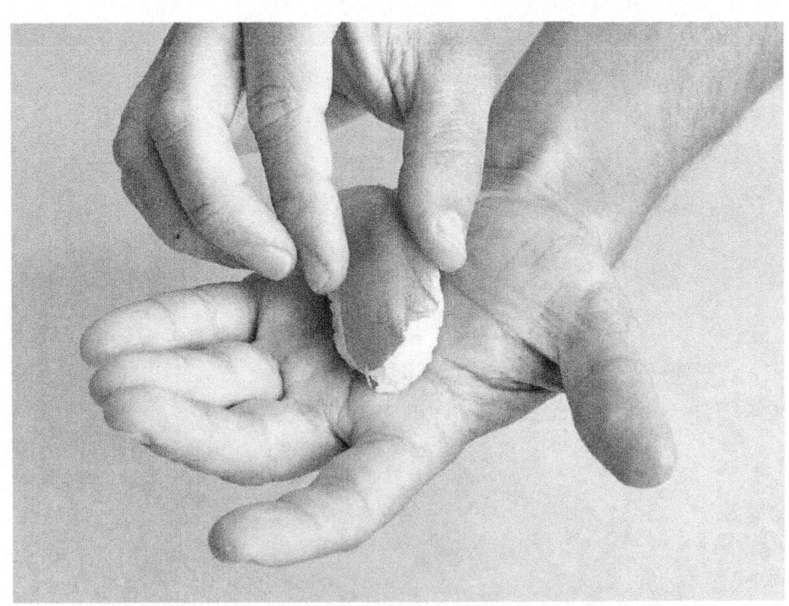

2. Place a dash of wasabi on the center of the rice, cover with a slice of tuna, gently press the fish down on the rice, and transfer it to a serving plate. Repeat with the remaining rice, wasabi, and tuna.

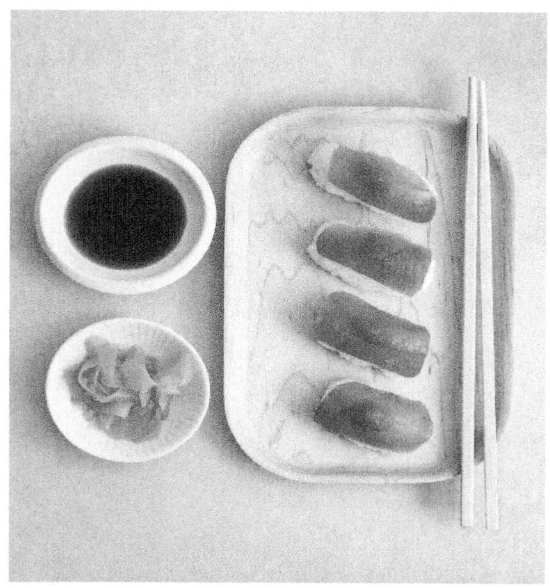

3. Put the ginger on the corner of the plate (or in a small bowl alongside) and serve with a small, shallow dish of soy sauce for each person.

COOKING TIP: Wet your hands and the tablespoon before touching the sushi rice, so the rice doesn't stick.

INGREDIENT TIP: If you prefer not to use wasabi, skip that part of the step.

Japanese Egg Omelet Nigiri

GLUTEN-FREE, NUT-FREE, KID FRIENDLY, VEGETARIAN

This is a popular nigiri in sushi restaurants despite the fact that it is no seafood sushi. Also, most kids love it because egg omelets are a dish that kids usually enjoy, and the sushi is served without wasabi. The egg omelet is usually shaky on the sushi rice, so it is fastened using a nori strip. But traditionally, this nigiri sushi is served either with and without the nori. When the omelet stays firmly on top of the rice, it is not necessary to use nori.

Yield: 10 pieces

Prep time: 20 minutes

Cook time: 12 minutes

Ingredients:

- Japanese Egg Omelet cut crosswise into ten ½-inch-wide pieces
- 2 cups Sushi Rice
- Soy sauce (gluten-free if necessary)
- 10 (½-by-4-inch) nori strips

Directions:

1. Divide the rice into 10 portions, place each into wet hands, and make it into a flat football shape.
2. Place a piece of omelet on each piece of shaped rice.
3. Fasten the omelet in place using one nori strip crossways with the seam on the bottom. Place the sushi seam-side down on a serving plate. Repeat with the remaining rice, omelet pieces, and nori strips.
4. Serve with a small, shallow dish of soy sauce for each person.

Salmon Nigiri with Marinated Sweet Onion

GLUTEN-FREE, NUT-FREE, PESCATARIAN

This traditional salmon nigiri sushi is eaten with marinated onion rather than wasabi. The onion's pungent component, which comes from allyl sulfide, refreshes the palate when it is eaten with rich and fatty-tasting fish. Also, the allyl sulfide helps our bodies absorb vitamin B_1, which enables the body to use carbohydrates for energy.

The combination of salmon and onion is great because salmon is high in vitamin B_1.

Yield: 10 to 12 pieces

Prep time: 20 minutes

Cook time: 8 minutes

Ingredients:

- ½ pound sashimi-grade salmon, sliced
- Soy sauce (gluten-free if necessary)
- 2 cups Sushi Rice
- ¼ cup Marinated Sweet Onion

Directions:

1. Scoop 1 heaping tablespoon of sushi rice on your wet hand and make it into a flat football shape.
2. Place a slice of salmon on the rice and top with 1 teaspoon of onion. Repeat with the remaining rice, salmon, and onion.
3. Serve with a small, shallow dish of soy sauce for each person.

Boiled Shrimp Nigiri

GLUTEN-FREE, NUT-FREE, PESCATARIAN

The tail-on pink-shrimp makes this dish great looking. To make boiled nigiri sushi shrimp perfectly, you should choose tail-on, un-deveined, medium-size shrimp. Store-bought deveined shrimp is usually slit on the backside, which makes it impossible to butterfly the shrimp from the belly side. You can butterfly the shrimp from the backside, but the tail becomes upswept (meaning upside down) when it lays on the rice. Large shrimp can be used as nigiri sushi shrimp, but it is a little bit difficult to butterfly them because of their thickness.

Yield: 10 pieces

Prep time: 35 minutes

Cook time: 5 minutes

Ingredients:

- 2 cups Sushi Rice
- Soy sauce (gluten-free if necessary)
- Wasabi
- 10 medium shell-on, tail-on shrimp, prepared

Directions:

1. Fill a deep pan with water and bring it to a boil over high heat.
2. Meanwhile, slowly insert a skewer in the shrimp from head to tail beneath the shell on the belly (leg) side to prevent it from curling when cooked. Boil five skewered shrimp at a time over medium heat for 2 to 3 minutes, or until they turn pink.
3. Once it cools enough to handle, remove the shell and legs, and make an incision from the belly side and butterfly. After it is opened, if you see back veins, gently remove them.

4. Divide the rice into 10 portions. With wet hands, form each portion into a flat football shape.
5. Place a dash of wasabi on the center of the rice and cover it with a piece of shrimp. Repeat with the remaining rice, wasabi, and shrimp.
6. Serve with a small, shallow dish of soy sauce for each person.

COOKING TIP: You can devein shrimp using a toothpick without cutting, but this requires a little technique. For nigiri shrimp, it is easiest to devein after butterflying.

Scallop Nigiri

GLUTEN-FREE, NUT-FREE, PESCATARIAN

As with the scallop sashimi dish, scallop nigiri sushi is served with natural sea salt. This is a special way to eat it, but only when the scallop is very fresh. You can use soy sauce instead of salt if you prefer the taste or if the scallop is not very fresh. The scallop is butterflied and placed on top of the sushi rice. If you halve the scallop by accident, you can lay half the sliced scallop overlapping the edge of the other half on the rice.

Yield: 10 pieces

Prep time: 20 minutes

Ingredients:

- 2 tablespoons Pickled Sushi Ginger
- Wasabi
- 2 cups Sushi Rice
- 10 scallops, butterflied
- Natural sea salt

Directions:

1. Divide the rice into 10 portions, place each into wet hands, and make it into a flat football shape.

2. Place a dash of wasabi on the center of the rice, cover with a scallop, and transfer to a serving plate. Repeat with the remaining rice, wasabi, and scallops.

3. Put the ginger on the corner of the plate and serve with a small, shallow dish of salt for each person.

Chicken Teriyaki Nigiri

GLUTEN-FREE, NUT-FREE, KID FRIENDLY

This nigiri is very popular with kids. Chicken teriyaki is a common food from Japan. It has a sweet-savory taste and a juicy, soft texture. Homemade chicken teriyaki takes only 15 minutes using one skillet. The key to making juicy chicken in a short amount of time is panfrying and pan-steaming the chicken with cooking sake. If you prefer, you can use any kind of broth instead of sake. Because of the shape of the sliced chicken, you need to fasten the chicken onto the sushi rice using a nori strip.

Yield: 10 to 12 pieces

Prep time: 25 minutes

Cook time: 15 minutes

Ingredients:

- 1 tablespoon vegetable oil
- 2 medium boneless, skinless chicken thighs
- ½ tablespoon cooking sake, plus 1 teaspoon
- ½ tablespoon soy sauce (gluten-free if necessary)
- ½ tablespoon mirin
- ½ teaspoon sugar

- 2 cups Sushi Rice
- 10 (½-by-4-inch) nori strips

Directions:

1. In a skillet, heat the vegetable oil over medium heat until it shimmers. Add the chicken and cook for 4 minutes. Flip the chicken, add ½ tablespoon of cooking sake, cover the skillet, and reduce the heat to low. Steam the chicken for 3 minutes.

2. Add the remaining 1 teaspoon of cooking sake, the soy sauce, mirin, and sugar. Increase the heat to medium and simmer for 6 minutes, turning the chicken occasionally and using a spoon to baste it with the sauce frequently, until the sauce is almost completely reduced. Let it cool and slice into ½-inch-thick pieces.

3. Scoop 1 heaping tablespoon of sushi rice onto your wet hand and make it into a flat football shape. Place a piece of chicken on the rice. Fasten the chicken in place using 1 nori strip crossways with the seam on the bottom. Place the sushi seam-side down on a serving plate. Repeat with the remaining rice, chicken, and nori.

Beef with Scallion Nigiri

GLUTEN-FREE, NUT-FREE

Although traditional sushi is a combination of seafood and rice, there are now many other types of sushi. This beef nigiri has become very popular in sushi restaurants in Japan. The beef is seasoned with soy sauce and wasabi, so the taste goes really well with sushi rice. It is also a great idea to use roasted beef instead of sautéed beef if you like.

Yield: 10 to 12 pieces

Prep time: 20 minutes

Cook time: 10 minutes

Ingredients:

- 2 scallions, both white and green parts, chopped
- ¼ teaspoon wasabi
- 6 ounces sirloin steak, chuck steak, or rib-eye steak, sliced into 1-by-2-inch pieces, ¼ to ½ inch thick
- 2 tablespoon soy sauce (gluten-free if necessary)
- 2 cups Sushi Rice

Directions:

1. Heat a dry skillet over medium heat for a few minutes, then cook the beef on one side for 3 to 4 minutes.
2. Meanwhile, mix the wasabi and soy sauce.
3. Flip the beef, add the sauce, and cook for another 3 to 4 minutes until it turns brown. Set aside.
4. Scoop 1 heaping tablespoon of sushi rice on your wet hand and make it into a flat football shape. Repeat with the remaining rice.
5. Once the beef cools enough to handle, place a piece on each mound of shaped rice, transfer to a serving dish, and sprinkle with the scallions.

COOKING TIP: If the skillet is too small to cook all the beef at once, cook it in batches.

INGREDIENT TIP: If you use leaner meat, heat ½ tablespoon oil in the skillet until it shimmers before adding the beef to the pan.

Spam Nigiri

GLUTEN-FREE, NUT-FREE, KID FRIENDLY

Believe it or not, Spam is very popular in Japan, especially in the Okinawa islands, because the main island has many US military bases. Spam is a great emergency food because under the right conditions, it lasts three years from the production date, and it can be eaten on its own. In fact, in the aftermath of the Great East Japan Earthquake (2011), Spam was issued for disaster victims. Japanese people use Spam mainly as an ingredient for sautéed dishes, rice balls, sandwiches, and fried rice.

Yield: 10 pieces

Prep time: 25 minutes

Cook time: 5 minutes

Ingredients:

- 10 (½-by-4-inch) nori strips
- 2 cups Sushi Rice
- 1 (12-ounce) can Spam, sliced into 10 pieces

Directions:

1. Heat a dry skillet over medium heat for a few minutes, then cook the Spam for 3 to 4 minutes, flipping halfway through the cooking time, until it is browned.

2. Divide the rice into 10 portions. Place each portion into wet hands, and make it into a flat football shape.

3. Fasten the Spam in place using 1 nori strip crossways with the seam on the bottom. Place the sushi seam-side down on a serving plate. Repeat with the remaining rice, Spam, and nori.

3.3 Gunkanmaki sushi

Buttery Corn Gunkanmaki

GLUTEN-FREE, NUT-FREE, VEGETARIAN, KID FRIENDLY

This dish is very popular among children. It's not a typical dish, but you will find this sushi at most conveyor-belt sushi restaurants in Japan today. To the cup, butter and soy sauce provide a rich taste. I use frozen corn, but for this recipe, fresh corn may also be used. In that scenario, instead, cook the corn for around 5 minutes over medium-low heat.

Yield: 10 to 12 pieces

Prep time: 30 minutes

Cook time: 10 minutes

Ingredients:

- 2 tablespoons butter or margarine
- 1 cup frozen sweet corn kernels
- 2 tablespoons soy sauce (gluten-free if necessary)
- 2 cups Sushi Rice
- 2 whole nori sheets

Directions:

1. In a skillet, melt the butter over medium-high heat. Add the corn and stir-fry for about 5 minutes to evaporate the water from the frozen corn. Add the soy sauce and stir for 1 minute.
2. Scoop 1 heaping tablespoon of sushi rice on your wet hand and form it into a flat football shape.
3. Wrap a strip of nori around the sides of the rice, shiny-side out, creating a tiny collar all around the rice. It is okay that the edge of the nori strip doesn't stick firmly.
4. Put 1 tablespoon of the corn on top. Repeat with the remaining rice, nori, and corn.

Minced Tuna and Scallion (Negitoro) Gunkanmaki

GLUTEN-FREE, NUT-FREE, PESCATARIAN

In Japanese, negitoro means scallion (Negi) and fatty tuna (toro). While lean tuna is used in the recipe, it is named toro since minced tuna has a fluffy texture, and like toro, it appears to melt in your mouth. For the

Japanese dish, tuna is often flavored with mayonnaise, but here I introduce you to the conventional version using soy sauce.

Yield: 12 pieces

Prep time: 40 minutes

Cook time: 15 minutes

Ingredients:

- ½ pound sashimi-grade tuna
- 1 tablespoon soy sauce (gluten-free if necessary)
- 2 cups Sushi Rice
- 2 whole nori sheets, cut
- 1 scallion, both white and green parts, chopped

Directions:

1. Cut the tuna into small pieces and mince finely. Place in a bowl, mix in the soy sauce and divide into 12 equal portions.

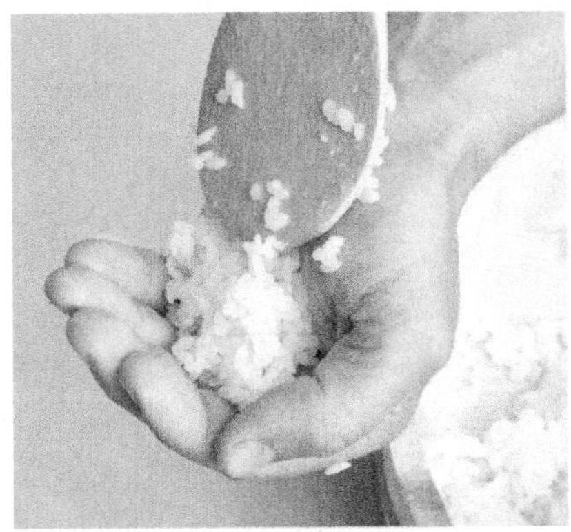

2. Divide the rice into 12 portions, place each portion into your wet hand, and make it into a flat football shape.

3. Wrap a strip of nori around the sides of the rice, shiny-side out, creating a tiny collar all around the rice. It is okay that the edge of the nori strip doesn't stick firmly.

4. Put one portion of the tuna mixture on the rice and top with some chopped scallion. Repeat with the remaining rice, nori, tuna, and scallions.

Salmon Roe (Ikura) Gunkanmaki

GLUTEN-FREE, NUT-FREE, PESCATARIAN

In Japanese, Gunkan means "warship." Gunkanmaki is so-called since the shape of the warship is perfect for carrying ingredients in some other manner that would be quickly dropped. Salmon roe (ikura) tastes abundant in umami. It is rich in protein, vitamins, and magnesium, which are healthy. Most specifically, ikura is one of the strongest Arginine rich foods in fish and shellfish that are considered to improve the immune system. It's good, but it's still high in cholesterol and calories, so make sure you just consume a tiny amount.

Yield: 10 to 12 pieces

Prep time: 30 minutes

Cook time: 15 minutes

Ingredients:

- 2 whole nori sheets, cut.
- 2 cups Sushi Rice
- 7 ounces salmon roe

Directions:

1. Scoop 1 heaping tablespoon of sushi rice on your wet hand and form it into a flat football shape.
2. Wrap a strip of nori around the sides of the rice, shiny-side out, creating a tiny collar all around the rice. It is okay that the edge of the nori strip doesn't stick firmly.
3. Place 1 tablespoon of salmon roe on top of the rice. Repeat with the remaining rice, nori, and salmon roe.

Lemony Crabmeat Gunkanmaki

GLUTEN-FREE, NUT-FREE, PESCATARIAN

As lump crab is hard to use in other forms of sushi, this gunkanmaki is perfect for consuming crabmeat as a sushi bowl. The crab meat in this dish is flavored with lemon juice, salt, and pepper. It can be seasoned, if you like, with mayonnaise instead of lemon juice. The sliced cucumber gives the sushi good contact. The slice of cucumber in gunkanmaki is often used if appropriate to brush the sushi with soy sauce; just dip the edge of the cucumber in soy sauce and brush it over the sushi.

Yield: 10 to 12 pieces

Prep time: 40 minutes

Cook time: 20 minutes

Ingredients:

- 1 baby cucumber, sliced diagonally
- 2 Salt
- Juice of ½ lemon
- 1 (4¼-ounce) can lump crabmeat, drained
- Freshly ground black pepper

- 2 cups Sushi Rice
- 2 whole nori sheets, cut

Directions:

1. In a bowl, whisk together the crabmeat, a pinch of salt and pepper, and lemon juice. Taste and add more salt and pepper as needed.
2. Scoop 1 heaping tablespoon of sushi rice on your wet hand and form into a flat football shape.
3. Wrap a strip of nori around the sides of the rice, shiny-side out, creating a tiny collar all around the rice. It is okay that the edge of the nori strip doesn't stick firmly.
4. Set 1 or 2 pieces of sliced cucumber on the edge of the rice, and put 2 teaspoons of the crabmeat on the rice. Repeat with the remaining rice, nori, cucumber, and crabmeat.

Corn and Tuna with Mayo Gunkanmaki

NUT-FREE, PESCATARIAN, KID FRIENDLY

In Japan, this mixture of corn and tuna is very common. There is canned food available in Japan, which is a combination of tuna and maize. For sautéed recipes, lettuce, spaghetti, pizza, and rice dishes, we use it. The corn and tuna are flavored with mayonnaise in this recipe. In my fridge, I still have frozen corn because it is really convenient. I still use it for this recipe; however, you may substitute kernels of fresh maize. This sushi is prepared and is loved by people of all ages in several sushi restaurants.

Yield: 10 to 12 pieces

Prep time: 30 minutes

Cook time: 10 minutes

Ingredients:

- ½ cup frozen sweet corn kernels
- 1 (5-ounce) can tuna packed in water, drained
- 2 tablespoons mayonnaise
- Salt
- Freshly ground black pepper

- 2 cups Sushi Rice
- 2 whole nori sheets

Directions

1. In a small microwave-safe bowl, microwave the frozen corn, covered, for about 50 seconds.
2. In a small bowl, mix the corn, tuna, and mayonnaise. Taste and season with salt and pepper as needed.
3. Scoop 1 heaping tablespoon of sushi rice on your wet hand and form it into a flat football shape.
4. Wrap a strip of nori around the sides of the rice, shiny-side out, creating a tiny collar all around the rice. It is okay that the edge of the nori strip doesn't stick firmly. Put 1 tablespoon of the tuna mixture on top. Repeat with the remaining rice, nori, and tuna mixture.

3.4 Temari sushi

Marinated Tuna (Zuke-Maguro) Temari

GLUTEN-FREE, NUT-FREE, PESCATARIAN

When refrigerators were not commonly used, Zuke was the name of one of the popular methods of preserving fresh tuna. Nowadays, it is found in sushi and rice bowls as an ingredient. In a mildly sweet sauce created from a combination of soy sauce, cooking sake, and mirin, the tuna is marinated, but it does not need to be eaten with some sauce.

Yield: 12 pieces

Prep time: 55 minutes

Cook time: 5 minutes

Ingredients:

- 8 ounces sashimi-grade tuna, sliced thinly
- 2 scallions, both white and green parts, chopped
- 2 cups Sushi Rice
- Roasted white sesame seeds
- 2 tablespoons cooking sake

- 2 tablespoons mirin
- 4 tablespoons soy sauce (gluten-free if necessary)

Directions:

1. In a small saucepan, stir together the soy sauce, cooking sake, and mirin. Bring the mixture to a boil over medium-high heat. Turn the heat to low and cook for 3 minutes. Turn off the heat, allow the pan to cool for 1 or 2 minutes, and transfer to the refrigerator and let it cool for about 15 minutes.
2. After cooling, remove the pan from the refrigerator, add the tuna, and flip until it is coated completely with the sauce. Marinate for 20 minutes in the refrigerator.
3. On a piece of plastic wrap (about 6 by 6 inches), place 1 slice of marinated tuna; put 1 heaping tablespoon of the rice on the tuna.
4. Hold up the four corners of the wrap with one hand and twist the sushi tightly with the other hand to make a ball shape. Transfer the sushi to a serving plate. Repeat with the remaining tuna slices and rice. Sprinkle with the sesame seeds and scallions.

Smoked Salmon Temari with Cucumber

GLUTEN-FREE, NUT-FREE, PESCATARIAN

In recent years, Temari sushi, which is pronounced "Temari-zushi" in Japanese, was made, but no one is sure exactly when. There is a belief that the birthplace of Temari sushi in Kyoto, Japan's ancient imperial city. Without spreading the mouth wide, Temari sushi has a thin circular ball form and can be consumed. It could be based on an ancient idea that it was disgraceful conduct to take big bites or joke with a wide-open mouth. Lately, since it is a no-muss-no-fuss dish that is very simple to form using plastic wrap or damp cheesecloth, it is also popular as a homemade sushi dish.

Yield: 12 pieces

Prep time: 25 minutes

Cook time: 15 minutes

Ingredients:

- 2 cups Sushi Rice
- Baby cucumber thinly sliced lengthwise

- 12 slices smoked salmon slices, each 2 to 3 inches long

Directions:

1. On a 6-by-6-inch piece of plastic wrap or damp cheesecloth, place 1 slice of smoked salmon. Scoop 1 heaping tablespoon of rice on the salmon.

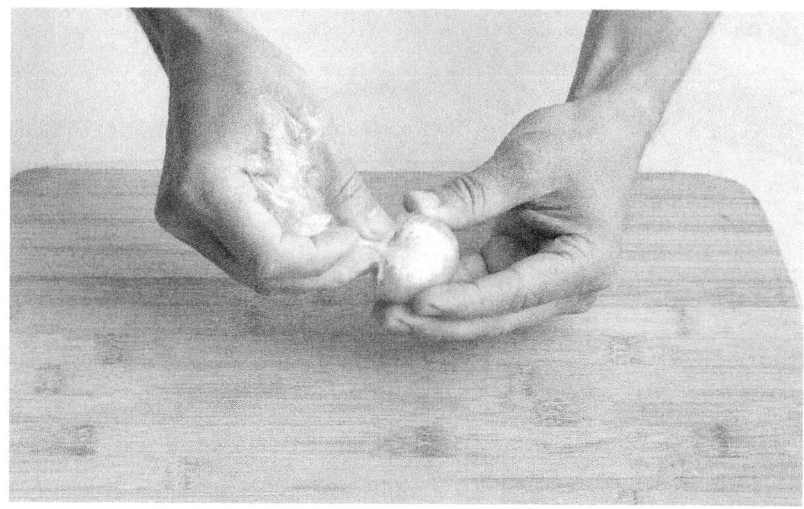

2. Hold up the four corners of the wrapper with one hand and twist the sushi tightly with the other hand to make a ball shape. Transfer the sushi to a serving plate. Repeat with the remaining salmon slices and rice.

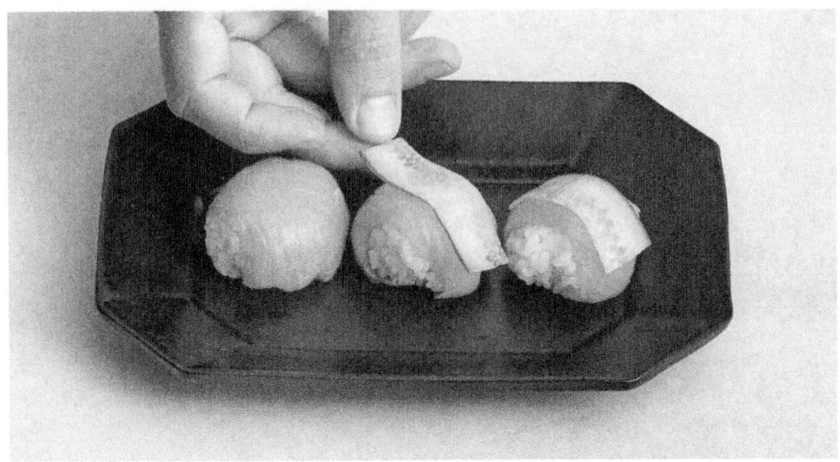

3. Top each piece of sushi with one slice of cucumber. The sushi can be eaten on its own.

INGREDIENT TIP: If you use cheesecloth to shape the sushi, you can keep rice from sticking to it by wringing out the cloth with water after every 2 or 3 pieces you make.

SERVING TIP: Smoked salmon has a delicious taste and flavor, so the sushi can be eaten on its own. Serve with a small, shallow dish of soy sauce, if necessary.

Egg and Salmon Roe Temari

GLUTEN-FREE, NUT-FREE, PESCATARIAN

Temari is the name of a typical hand-sized, colorful ball that is Japanese art. Therefore, Temari sushi is thin, nice, and formed like a ball. With a rice ball covered in thin fried eggs and filled with salmon roe, this recipe is a hallmark of Temari sushi. It has bright yellow and orange shades, and the rice's ball form and salmon roe complement very well. At any gathering, this Temari sushi recipe will take center stage.

Yield: 10 pieces

Prep time: 25 minutes

Cook time: 10 minutes

Ingredients:

- Nonstick cooking spray
- 1 teaspoon water
- 2 eggs, beaten
- 3 tablespoons salmon roe
- 3 cups Sushi Rice
- 1 teaspoon cornstarch

Directions:

1. In a small bowl, whisk together the cornstarch and water. Mix the cornstarch mixture into the beaten eggs.

2. Heat a 10-inch skillet over medium-high heat and coat with cooking spray. Pour half of the egg mixture into the skillet and spread the egg all over the surface of the pan to make a thin layer. Cook over low heat for about 3 minutes, gently flipping halfway through the cooking time with a rubber spatula. Make another thin fried egg with the remaining egg mixture.

3. Transfer the fried eggs to a cutting board, cut each lengthwise into three equal pieces, then cut each piece crosswise into three pieces to create 18 approximately equal-sized pieces.

4. On a 6-by-6-inch piece of plastic wrap or damp cheesecloth, place 1 piece of egg and scoop 1 heaping tablespoon of the rice on the egg.

5. Hold up the four corners of the wrapper with one hand and twist the sushi tightly with the other hand

to make a ball shape. Transfer the sushi to a serving plate. Repeat with the remaining egg pieces and rice.

6. Top each sushi with ½ teaspoon of salmon roe.

COOKING TIP: The cornstarch keeps the thin fried egg from tearing. However, when it is cooked too long, the egg crisps and can shatter.

3.5 Temaki sushi

Traditional Hand-Rolled Sushi

GLUTEN-FREE, NUT-FREE, PESCATARIAN

Typical handmade sushi is hand-rolled sushi, which in Japanese is called temaki. There's no need for a specific rolling technique because any ingredients you want can be used. I use sashimi tuna and salmon in this recipe, both of which are the most common hand-rolled sushi ingredients. Some unseasoned ingredients are dipped in soy sauce for temaki sushi recipes before being set on the rice, so the sushi can be eaten without soy sauce. Substitute Japanese basil (shiso) for the parsley if you can get it. Put a splash of wasabi on the rice if you like using wasabi.

Yield: 8 rolls

Prep time: 40 minutes

Cook time: 20 minutes

Ingredients:

- Parsley
- 2 cups Sushi Rice
- ¼ pound sashimi-grade salmon, sliced
- 2 whole nori sheets
- ¼ pound sashimi-grade tuna, sliced
- Soy sauce (gluten-free if necessary)

Directions:

1. Put a piece of nori on your palm and spread 2 tablespoons of rice on it with a wet spoon.

2. Dip a piece of tuna and salmon in soy sauce, and arrange each piece with 1 sprig of parsley diagonally across the middle of the rice. Roll into a cone shape. Repeat with the remaining nori, rice, and tuna and salmon slices.

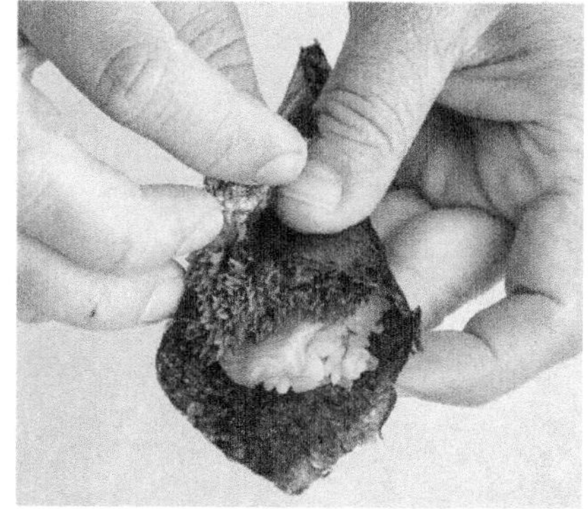

Beef with Lettuce Temaki

GLUTEN-FREE, NUT-FREE

This sushi idea comes from Korean cuisine and consists of sautéed beef wrapped with lettuce. In this recipe, the vinegar-marinated sweet onion is placed on top of the beef, so it has a very fresh taste. You could even use the lettuce as a wrapper instead of nori. Spread the rice on the lettuce, place the ingredients on the rice, and roll-up. This is so delicious! As just described, temaki recipes are unlimited because they are easy to roll, and there are no traditional rules. If you held a temaki sushi party, tons of recipes could be created by your guests!

Yield: 8 rolls

Prep time: 40 minutes

Cook time: 10 minutes

Ingredients:

- 4 ounces sirloin steak, chuck steak, or rib-eye steak, cut into ½-inch-thick and 2½-inchlong stick
- Salt
- Freshly ground black pepper

- 2 whole nori sheets,
- 2 cups Sushi Rice
- 2 green leaf lettuce leaves, torn into palm-size pieces ¼ cup Marinated Sweet Onion

Directions:

1. Heat a dry skillet over medium heat for a few minutes, and cook the beef for about 7 minutes or until it turns brown. Season with the salt and pepper halfway through the cooking time. Set aside.
2. Put a piece of nori in your palm, spread 2 tablespoons of the rice over it with a wet spoon, and place the lettuce on the rice.
3. Arrange a stack of beef and about ½ tablespoon of onion diagonally across the middle of the lettuce. Roll into a cone shape.

Repeat with the remaining nori, rice, and filling.

Salad Temaki

NUT-FREE, PESCATARIAN

A typical temaki sushi recipe that doesn't contain any fresh fish is this salad hand roll. The cucumber brings to the sushi a beautiful crunchy feel. Leg-style imitation crabmeat is really convenient and quick to use, although, with this recipe, flake-style can also be used if you can't locate it. Using two pieces of meat in that case for each hand-rolled sushi. For all hand-rolled sushi recipes, I use square nori. Any other dishes use rectangular nori with the same volume of rice, which is two times bigger than a rectangle. A decent cone form with rectangular nori is simple to produce, but the sushi has more nori and is slightly more difficult to bite and chew than this recipe.

Yield: 8 rolls

Prep time: 40 minutes

Cook time: 15 minutes

Ingredients:

- 2 cups Sushi Rice
- Japanese Egg Omelet

- 8 teaspoons mayonnaise
- 2 whole nori sheets, cut
- 1 baby cucumber, cut into thin strips
- 8 pieces leg-style imitation crabmeat

Directions:

1. Cut the omelet into quarters lengthwise and halve each quarter crosswise. Set aside.
2. Put a piece of nori in your palm and spread 2 tablespoons of the rice over it with a wet spoon.
3. Arrange 1 piece of omelet, 1 piece of imitation crabmeat, and some sliced cucumber diagonally across the middle of the rice. Put 1 teaspoon of mayonnaise on the cucumber. Roll into a cone shape.

   Repeat with the remaining nori, rice, and filling.

Chapter 4: Maki Rolls

Most traditional sushi rolls have three basic features: the exteriors is nori, the form is completely oval, and without toppings, they are eaten. Here I'm going to show you how to make traditional and non-traditional sushi rolls that are either well known or brand fresh.

4.1 Cucumber Roll (Kappamaki)

GLUTEN-FREE, NUT-FREE, VEGAN

The cucumber roll was created in Japan during a food shortage after World War II. Unexpectedly it became very popular, even though it doesn't include fresh seafood. The Japanese call this roll kappamaki. Kappa is a monster in Japanese folklore, and many kappa stories say the kappa likes to eat cucumber, so it is named kappamaki. Although the recipe notes that it takes 40 minutes to prepare, when you get used to rolling sushi, it will become faster.

Yield: 4 thin rolls or 24 pieces

Prep time: 40 minutes

Cook time: 15 minutes

Ingredients:

- 2 whole nori sheets, halved
- 2 cups Sushi Rice
- 2 baby cucumbers
- Soy sauce (gluten-free if necessary)

Directions:

1. Put the makisu on a work surface and place one piece of nori on it, shiny-side down. Spread ½ cup of sushi rice evenly over the nori, leaving a ½-inch border visible.

2. Place 2 sticks of cucumber across the middle of the rice.

3. Begin rolling by picking up the edge of the makisu and nori closest to you and folding it over the cucumber. Hold the roll tightly to form a good shape. Let it sit, seam-side down, for 2 minutes or until the nori sticks firmly. Make three more rolls with the remaining nori, rice, and filling.

4. Cut each sushi roll into 6 pieces with a knife that is wiped on a clean, damp kitchen towel before each cut. Transfer to a serving plate. Serve with a small shallow dish of soy sauce for each person.

COOKING TIP: This thin sushi roll can also be shaped as a square, which is a little bit easier to make. Just gently push the sides of the sushi roll against the work surface to make four flat faces while you hold the roll tightly.

4.2 Tuna Roll (Tekkamaki)

GLUTEN-FREE, NUT-FREE, PESCATARIAN

This thin tuna roll is a traditional and very popular dish. In Tokyo, this dish is very small and nori-side out, which makes it a handy finger food for a quick lunch. To keep things clean, I recommend using the edge of the paddle to spread the rice. Be sure to wet the paddle between each roll.

Yield: 4 thin rolls or 24 pieces

Prep time: 40 minutes

Cook time: 20 minutes

Ingredients:

- 2 whole nori sheets, halved
- 2 cups Sushi Rice
- Wasabi
- 4 ounces sashimi-grade tuna
- Soy sauce (gluten-free if necessary)

Directions:

1. Put the makisu on a work surface and place one piece of nori on it, shiny-side down. Spread ½ cup of sushi rice evenly over the nori, leaving a ½-inch border visible.

2. With your finger, spread a small amount of wasabi across the middle of the rice, then lay 3 pieces of the tuna on the wasabi.

3. Begin rolling by picking up the edge of the makisu and nori closest to you and folding it over the tuna. Hold the roll tightly to form a good shape. Let it sit seam-side down for 2 minutes or until the nori sticks firmly. Make three more rolls with the remaining nori, rice, and filling.

4. Cut each sushi roll into 6 pieces with a knife that is wiped on a clean, damp kitchen towel before each cut. Transfer to a serving plate. Serve with a small shallow dish of soy sauce for each person.

COOKING TIP: Once the near side of the rice attaches to the far side of the rice, hold the roll tightly to encourage a good shape and keep it from falling apart. Then keep rolling while holding just the makisu.

4.3 Spicy Tuna Roll

GLUTEN-FREE, NUT-FREE, PESCATARIAN

The spicy tuna roll is a novel creation and has become incredibly popular all over the world. But you won't find this role in Japan. The key to making good-looking rice-side-out rolls is to place a piece of plastic wrap or parchment paper (about the same size as the makisu) on the rice and press lightly before flipping the rollover. This ensures that the rice and nori stick together nicely, which makes rolling and shaping easier.

Yield: 2 big rolls or 12 pieces

Prep time: 40 minutes

Cook time: 10 minutes

Ingredients:

- 2 whole nori sheets
- 2 cups Sushi Rice
- 4 tablespoons roasted sesame seeds
- 1½ tablespoons Spicy Mayonnaise Sauce
- 4 ounces sashimi-grade tuna
- 1 baby cucumber

Directions:

1. Layout the makisu on a work surface and place one piece of nori on it, shiny-side down. Spread 1 cup of sushi rice evenly over the nori. Sprinkle the rice with 2 tablespoons of sesame seeds.

2. Place a piece of plastic wrap or parchment paper (about the same size as the makisu) on the rice and flip, so now the nori side is up.

3. Spread about ½ tablespoon of the mayonnaise sauce in a line across the middle of the nori. Lay half of the tuna and 2 sticks of cucumber on the sauce.

4. Begin rolling by picking up the edge of the makisu and nori closest to you and folding it over the ingredients. Hold the roll tightly to form a good shape. Let it sit, seam-side down, for 2 minutes. Make three more rolls with the remaining nori, rice, sesame seeds, and filling.

5. Cut each sushi roll into 6 pieces with a knife that is wiped on a clean, damp kitchen towel before each cut. Transfer to a serving plate and put a little of the remaining ½ tablespoon of mayonnaise sauce on top of each piece.

4.4 California Roll

NUT-FREE, PESCATARIAN

This may be the first sushi roll ever created by a Japanese sushi chef in the United States. The key to making a great California roll, which has the rice side out, is to spread rice all over the nori without leaving any uncovered. In this recipe, 1 cup of sushi rice is used on one whole nori. This is the perfect amount for making tight sushi rolls that won't break apart.

Yield: 2 big rolls or 12 pieces

Prep time: 25 minutes

Cook time: 13 minutes

Ingredients:

- 2 whole nori sheets
- 2 cups Sushi Rice
- 4 tablespoons roasted sesame seeds
- 1 tablespoon mayonnaise
- 2 pieces leg-style imitation crabmeat
- ½ avocado

Directions:

1. 1 baby cucumber, Layout the makisu on a work surface and place one sheet of nori on it, shiny-side down. Spread 1 cup of sushi rice evenly over the nori. Sprinkle the rice with 2 tablespoons of sesame seeds. Place a piece of plastic wrap or parchment paper (about the same size as the makisu) on the rice and flip so the nori side is up.
2. Spread ½ tablespoon of mayonnaise in a line across the middle of the nori. On the mayonnaise, place 2 pieces of the imitation crabmeat and half of the avocado slices. Below the imitation crabmeat, place 2 sticks of cucumber.
3. Begin rolling by picking up the edge of the makisu and nori closest to you and folding it over the ingredients. Let it sit, seam-side down, for 5 minutes at room temperature. Make another roll with the remaining nori, rice, sesame seeds, and filling.
4. Cut each sushi roll into 6 pieces with a knife that is wiped on a clean, damp kitchen towel before each cut.

COOKING TIP: If it is hard to spread 1 cup of the rice on the nori, add the rice little by little until you barely see the nori.

4.5 Traditional Big Roll (Futomaki)

GLUTEN-FREE, NUT-FREE, VEGETARIAN

This sushi roll is a big roll with the nori side out and typically filled with cooked vegetables and sometimes cooked seafood. The filling has a delicious sweet and savory taste, so there is no need to eat it with any sauce. In western Japan, where I was born and raised, there is a custom to eat this roll in silence while facing the year's lucky compass direction and wishing for perfect health.

Yield: 2 big rolls or 16 pieces

Prep time: 30 minutes

Cook time: 20 minutes

Ingredients:

- 2 large shiitake mushrooms, stemmed and sliced
- ½ carrot, cut into ¼-inch-thick sticks
- 10 spinach stalks
- 1 teaspoon Shimaya kombu dashi soup stock powder or any dashi powder you like
- ⅔ cup of water

- 2 tablespoon soy sauce (gluten-free if necessary)
- 1 tablespoon cooking sake
- 1 tablespoon mirin
- 1 tablespoon sugar
- 2 whole nori sheets
- 2 cups Sushi Rice
- Japanese Egg Omelet quartered lengthwise

Directions:

1. In a saucepan, stir together the mushrooms, carrot, spinach, dashi powder, water, soy sauce, sake, mirin, and sugar. Bring to a boil over medium heat, reduce the heat to maintain a simmer, and cook for 15 minutes. Let it cool and drain.
2. Layout the makisu on a work surface and place one sheet of nori on it, shiny-side down. Spread 1 cup of sushi rice evenly over the nori, leaving a 1-inch border visible.
3. Lay half of the shiitake mushrooms below the middle of the rice. Place half of the carrot sticks, 5 stalks of the spinach, and 2 sticks of the omelet over the

mushrooms. Fold back the ingredients that stick out from the side of the nori.

4. Begin rolling by picking up the edge of the makisu and nori closest to you and folding it over the ingredients. Hold the roll tightly to form a good shape. Let it sit, seam-side down, for 5 minutes at room temperature. Make another roll with the remaining nori, rice, and filling.

5. Cut each sushi roll into 8 pieces with a knife that is wiped on a clean, damp kitchen towel before each cut.

4.6 Boston Roll

GLUTEN-FREE, NUT-FREE, PESCATARIAN

If you want an eye-catching presentation, choose tail-on shrimp, so the tail sticks out from the sushi roll. I recommend using deveined shrimp, but if you can't find them, devein them yourself by cutting a shallow slit on the back of the shrimp and removing the vein.

Yield: 2 big rolls or 12 pieces

Prep time: 35 minutes

Cook time: 5 minutes

Ingredients:

- 4 medium or large tail-on shrimp, deveined
- 2 whole nori sheets
- 2 cups Sushi Rice
- 4 tablespoons roasted sesame seeds
- ½ avocado
- 1 baby cucumber
- Soy sauce (gluten-free if necessary)

Directions:

1. Fill a deep pan with water and bring it to a boil over high heat.
2. Meanwhile, carefully insert a skewer through the shrimp from head to tail to prevent them from curling when cooked. Place the skewer in the water and boil the shrimp over medium heat for 2 to 3 minutes until they turn pink. Once the shrimp are cool enough to handle, remove them from the skewer. Set aside.
3. Layout the makisu on a work surface and place one sheet of nori on it, shiny-side down. Spread 1 cup of sushi rice evenly over the nori. Sprinkle the rice with 2 tablespoons of sesame seeds.
4. Place a piece of plastic wrap or parchment paper (about the same size as the makisu) on the rice and flip so that the nori side is up.
5. Lay 2 shrimp, tails sticking out of the nori, across the middle of the rice, and place half of the avocado and 2 sticks of cucumber below the shrimp.
6. Pick up the edge of the makisu and nori closest to you and fold it into a tight jelly roll. Make another roll with the remaining nori, rice, sesame seeds, and filling.
7. Cut each sushi roll into 6 pieces and serve with soy sauce.

4.7 Philadelphia Roll

GLUTEN-FREE, NUT-FREE, PESCATARIAN

Salmon and cream cheese is a very popular combination in Japan. These are great ingredients for appetizer dishes, such as summer rolls and sushi rolls. Roll and hold this sushi gently because it consists of only soft fillings, unlike other sushi rolls. Be careful not to press the roll too tightly because the cheese may squeeze out from the side. Also, when you cut the roll, use a sharp knife and pull the knife toward you carefully in one cut, so the filling stays inside.

Yield: 4 thin rolls or 24 pieces

Prep time: 40 minutes

Cook time: 20 minutes

Ingredients:

- 2 whole nori sheets, halved
- 2 cups Sushi Rice
- 4 tablespoons roasted sesame seeds
- 4 ounces sashimi-grade salmon, cut

- ¾ (8-ounce) package cream cheese, cut into ½-inch-thick sticks
- 2 teaspoons wasabi
- Soy sauce (gluten-free if necessary)

Directions:

1. Layout the makisu on a work surface and place one piece of nori on it, shiny-side down. Spread ½ cup of sushi rice evenly over the nori. Sprinkle the rice with 1 tablespoon of sesame seeds.
2. Place a piece of plastic wrap or parchment paper (about the same size as the makisu) on the rice and flip so that the nori side is up.
3. Lay 3 pieces of the salmon across the middle of the nori, and arrange 1 or 2 pieces of the cream cheese sticks below the salmon.
4. Pick up the edge of the makisu and nori closest to you and roll it into a tight jelly roll. Let it sit, seam-side down, for 2 minutes. Make three more rolls with the remaining nori, rice, sesame seeds, and filling.

5. Cut each sushi roll into 6 pieces with a knife that is wiped on a clean, damp kitchen towel before each cut. Make the wasabi into a mound on the corner of a serving plate. Serve with a small, shallow dish of soy sauce for each person as needed.

4.8 Mexican Roll

NUT-FREE, PESCATARIAN

This roll topped with spicy Pico de Gallo will impress you with its irresistible taste and texture. The key to making great, crunchy tempura is to use cornstarch instead of flour. When the tempura gets cold, flour tempura becomes soggy, but cornstarch tempura keeps its crunchiness. To make perfect, straight shrimp tempura requires an extra step, which I will explain.

Yield: 2 big rolls or 12 pieces

Prep time: 35 minutes

Cook time: 5 minutes

Ingredients:

- 4 medium or large tail-on shrimp, peeled and deveined
- 1 tablespoon cornstarch
- Vegetable oil, for frying
- Tempura Batter
- 2 whole nori sheets

- 2 cups Sushi Rice
- 1 tablespoon Spicy Mayonnaise Sauce
- ½ avocado, cut
- 2 pieces leg-style imitation crabmeat, cut lengthwise
- 1 baby cucumber, cut
- ½ cup Pico de Gallo

Directions:

1. Cut a vertical slice on the belly of the shrimp. Place the shrimp belly-side down on a cutting board and press the shrimp lightly against the board to break the tight muscles and straighten. Dredge the shrimp in the cornstarch.
2. In a deep pan, heat 2 inches of vegetable oil over medium heat until it shimmers. Dip the shrimp into the batter, then fry for 2 minutes, occasionally flipping, until golden. Transfer to a wire rack to drain.
3. Put the makisu on a work surface. Place one sheet of nori on it, shiny-side down. Spread 1 cup of rice evenly over the nori. Place a piece of plastic wrap or

parchment paper (about the same size as the makisu) on the rice, and flip so the nori side is up.

4. Spread ½ tablespoon of the mayonnaise sauce in a line across the middle of the nori, and lay 2 shrimp pieces (tails sticking out of the nori) on the sauce. Place half of the avocado, 2 pieces of the imitation crab meat, and 2 sticks of cucumber below the shrimp.
5. Pick up the edge of the makisu and nori it into a tight jelly roll. Let it sit seam-side down for 5 minutes at room temperature. Make another roll with the remaining nori, rice, and filling.
6. Cut each sushi roll into 6 pieces and serve topped with Pico de Gallo.

COOKING TIP: To check whether the oil is hot enough to fry, drop in some batter. If it floats with bubbles, the oil is ready.

4.9 Alaskan Roll

GLUTEN-FREE, NUT-FREE, PESCATARIAN

This gorgeous roll is great for salmon lovers, with the perfect marriage of the creamy, mild taste of salmon and the fresh taste of asparagus. In this recipe, the asparagus is steamed in the microwave to make it easier to prepare. It can be grilled or pan-fried if you prefer.

Yield: 2 big rolls or 12 pieces

Prep time: 30 minutes

Cook time: 1 minute

Ingredients:

- 4 asparagus stalks, trimmed and rinsed
- 2 whole nori sheets
- 2 cups Sushi Rice
- 4 tablespoons roasted sesame seeds
- 4 ounces sashimi-grade salmon, cut
- ½ avocado
- 1 teaspoon wasabi
- 2 tablespoons salmon roe
- Soy sauce (gluten-free if necessary)

Directions:

1. On a microwave-safe plate, microwave the wet asparagus, covered, for about 40 seconds, until tender.
2. Layout the makisu on a work surface and place one piece of nori on it, shiny-side down. Spread 1 cup of sushi rice evenly over the nori. Sprinkle the rice with 2 tablespoons of sesame seeds.
3. Place a piece of plastic wrap or parchment paper (about the same size as the makisu) on the rice and flip so the nori side is up.
4. Lay 2 asparagus stalks across the middle of the nori. Arrange half of the salmon and half of the avocado below the asparagus.
5. Pick up the edge of the makisu and nori closest to you and roll it over the filling into a tight jelly roll. Let it sit, seam-side down, for 5 minutes at room temperature. Make another roll with the remaining nori, rice, sesame seeds, and filling.

Cut each sushi roll into 6 pieces, add a small wasabi mound on the corner of a serving plate and ½ teaspoon of salmon roe on each sushi piece, and serve with a small, shallow dish of soy sauce for each person.

4.10 Dragon Roll

GLUTEN-FREE, NUT-FREE, PESCATARIAN

The Dragon Roll's appearance is reminiscent of dragon scales. To decorate this roll, overlap the edges of the sliced avocado repeatedly. If you can find cooked eel, top the roll with alternating slices of eel and avocado. In addition, this roll is sprinkled with agedama (tempura batter bits) to add a crunchy texture. You can also use store-bought agedama instead of homemade.

Yield: 2 big rolls or 12 pieces

Prep time: 35 minutes

Cook time: 10 minutes

Ingredients:

- 2 whole nori sheets
- 2 cups Sushi Rice
- 4 ounces sashimi-grade tuna
- 1 baby cucumber
- 1 avocado,
- Tempura Batter Bits
- Spicy Mayonnaise Sauce

Directions:

1. Put the makisu on a work surface. Place one sheet of nori on it, shiny-side down. Spread 1 cup of sushi rice evenly over the nori. Place a piece of plastic wrap or parchment paper (about the same size as the makisu) on the rice and flip so the nori side is up.
2. Arrange half of the tuna across the middle of the nori, and place 2 sticks of cucumber below the tuna.
3. Pick up the edge of the makisu and nori into a tight jelly roll. Remove the wrap and makisu, place the roll seam-side down, and arrange half of the avocado diagonally over the roll to mimic the pattern of dragon scales. Cover the roll with the wrap and hold it tightly to make the avocado stick to the roll firmly. Let it sit for 5 minutes at room temperature. Make another roll with the remaining nori, rice, filling, and topping.
4. Cut each sushi roll into 6 pieces and serve with the batter bits sprinkled on top and a drizzle of the mayonnaise sauce.

SUBSTITUTION TIP: If you can get tobiko or masago, top each piece with about ¼ teaspoon of it instead of sprinkling with tempura batter bits.

4.11 Rainbow Roll

NUT-FREE, PESCATARIAN

Rainbow rolls usually include many kinds of raw seafood and are covered with colorful ingredients. In this recipe, I use sliced avocado and sliced smoked salmon as the topping ingredients. When my sushi roll is misshapen, I cover the roll with avocado, sliced sashimi, or sliced cucumber as a topping to enhance the visual effect.

Yield: 2 big rolls or 12 pieces

Prep time: 35 minutes

Cook time: 15 minutes

Ingredients:

- 2 whole nori sheets
- 2 cups Sushi Rice
- 4 ounces sashimi-grade tuna
- 2 pieces leg-style imitation crabmeat
- 1 baby cucumber
- 4 ounces sliced smoked salmon
- ½ avocado

Directions:

1. Place the makisu on a work surface. Place one sheet of nori on it, shiny-side down. Spread 1 cup of sushi rice evenly over the nori. Put a piece of plastic wrap or parchment paper (about the same size as the makisu) on the rice and flip so the nori side is up.
2. Lay half of the tuna across the middle of the nori and arrange 2 pieces of imitation crab meat and 2 sticks of cucumber below the tuna.
3. Pick up the edge of the makisu and nori into a tight jelly roll.
4. Remove the wrap and makisu, and place the roll seam-side down. Place half of the salmon and avocado slices diagonally next to each other over the roll. Cover the roll with the plastic wrap and hold it tightly to make the salmon and avocado stick to the roll firmly. Let it sit for 5 minutes at room temperature. Make another roll with the remaining nori, rice, filling, and topping.
5. Cut each sushi roll into 6 pieces and serve.

COOKING TIP: Smoked salmon and avocado are easy to tear when you cut. To avoid that, cut the roll through the wrapper (if you use plastic wrap) so the topping keeps its shape.

4.12 Seared Bonito (Katsuo-no tataki) Roll

GLUTEN-FREE, NUT-FREE, PESCATARIAN

This is a thin nori-side-out sushi roll filled with seared bonito, marinated sweet onion, and scallion. It seems like a traditional sushi roll, but the Japanese tend to eat seared bonito as a sashimi dish. Even though seared bonito is categorized as sashimi, and the middle part is raw, it is eaten not with wasabi but rather with grated ginger. Other common condiments for the bonito are garlic and Zingiber mioga (Japanese ginger).

Yield: 4 thin rolls or 24 pieces

Prep time: 40 minutes

Cook time: 5 minutes

Ingredients:

- 2 whole nori sheets, halved
- 2 cups Sushi Rice
- 4 ounces seared bonito, cut into ½-inch-thick and 2½-inch-long sticks
- 8 scallions, trimmed

- ½ cup Marinated Sweet Onion
- 1 tablespoon peeled, grated fresh ginger Ponzu Sauce

Directions:

1. Put the makisu on a work surface. Place one piece of nori on it, shiny-side down. Spread ½ cup of rice evenly over the nori, leaving a ½-inch border on the far side.
2. Place three pieces of the bonito and 2 scallions across the middle of the rice. Add 1 tablespoon of the onion on top.
3. Pick up the edge of the makisu and nori closest to you, attach the near edge of the rice to the far edge of the rice, and roll-up. Let it sit, seam-side down, for a few minutes. Make three more rolls with the remaining ingredients.
4. Cut each sushi roll into 6 pieces and serve with a small mound of ginger and a dash of Ponzu Sauce.

4.13 Shellfish Roll

GLUTEN-FREE, NUT-FREE, PESCATARIAN

This is an incredibly delicious roll, and you should thank the sea for its blessing! If you prefer, you can make this a true treat by adding lobster. Cut the lobster into ½-inch-thick sticks and add it with the other ingredients.

Yield: 2 big rolls or 12 pieces

Prep time: 35 minutes

Cook time: 5 minutes

Ingredients:

- 4 medium or large shrimp, tail on, deveined
- 2 whole nori sheets
- 2 cups Sushi Rice
- 4 tablespoons roasted sesame seeds
- Wasabi
- 1 baby cucumber
- 1 (4¼-ounce) can crabmeat, drained
- 6 sashimi-grade scallops, halved horizontally

- 2 tablespoons salmon roe
- Soy sauce (gluten-free if necessary)

Directions:

1. Fill a deep pan with water and bring it to a boil over high heat.
2. Skewer the shrimp from head to tail to prevent it from curling when cooked. Boil the shrimp over medium heat for 2 to 3 minutes, until it turns pink.
3. Put the makisu on a work surface and place one sheet of nori on it, shiny-side down. Spread 1 cup of rice evenly over the nori. Sprinkle the rice with 2 tablespoons of sesame seeds. Put a piece of plastic wrap or parchment paper (about the same size as the makisu) on the rice and flip so the nori side is up.
4. With your finger, spread a small amount of wasabi in a line across the middle of the nori. Place 2 shrimp pieces (tails sticking out of the nori) on the wasabi, and place 2 sticks of cucumber, 3 tablespoons of the crab, and 6 pieces of the scallop below the shrimp.

5. Pick up the edge of the makisu and nori closest to you, and roll into a tight jelly roll. Let it sit, seam-side down, for 5 minutes at room temperature. Make another roll with the remaining nori, rice, sesame seeds, and filling.

6. Cut each sushi roll into 6 pieces, top each piece with ½ teaspoon of the salmon roe, and serve with soy sauce.

4.14 Dynamite Roll

NUT-FREE, PESCATARIAN

Dynamite rolls usually consist of shrimp tempura and different kinds of vegetables. To create an impressive final presentation, choose tailon shrimp, so the tail sticks out from the end of the roll. Crispy fried onions add a great crunchy texture to the roll, and cucumber, sprouts, and red cabbage add color to the dish. You can use other vegetables, such as bell peppers, avocado, or celery, as additions or substitutions.

Yield: 2 big rolls or 12 pieces

Prep time: 40 minutes

Cook time: 5 minutes

Ingredients:

- 4 medium or large tail-on shrimp, deveined
- 1 tablespoon cornstarch
- Vegetable oil, for frying
- Tempura Batter
- 1 whole nori sheets

- 2 cups Sushi Rice
- 4 tablespoons roasted sesame seeds
- 2 tablespoons Spicy Mayonnaise Sauce, divided
- Baby cucumber, cut
- ½ cup bean sprouts washed
- ½ cup shredded red cabbage
- Sweet Eel Sauce
- ½ cup store-bought crispy fried onions

Directions:

1. Make small cuts vertically on the shrimp belly, place belly-side down on a cutting board, and press the shrimp lightly to straighten. Dredge the shrimp in the cornstarch.
2. In a deep pan, heat 2 inches of vegetable oil over medium heat until it shimmers. Dip the shrimp into the batter, then fry for 2 minutes, occasionally flipping, until golden. Transfer to a wire rack to drain.
3. Layout the makisu on a work surface and place one sheet of nori on top, shiny side down. Spread 1 cup of rice evenly over the nori, and sprinkle with 2

tablespoons of sesame seeds. Put a piece of plastic wrap or parchment paper (about the same size as the makisu) on the rice and flip so the nori side is up.

4. Spread about ½ tablespoon of the mayonnaise sauce across the middle of the nori. Place 2 shrimp, tails sticking out of the nori, on the sauce, and arrange 2 sticks of cucumber, ¼ cup of the sprouts, and ¼ cup of the cabbage below the shrimp.

5. Pick up the edge of the makisu and nori into a tight jelly roll. Let it sit, seam-side down, for 5 minutes at room temperature. Make another roll with the remaining nori, rice, sesame seeds, and filling.

Cut each sushi roll into 6 pieces and top each piece with a dash of mayonnaise sauce, a drizzle of the eel sauce, and a sprinkle of fried onions.

4.15 Cod Tempura Roll

GLUTEN-FREE, NUT-FREE, PESCATARIAN

Tempura is one of my favorite ways to eat cod. It has a soft texture and a deliciously light taste. When you cut cod into sticks, cut carefully because it will easily crumble. In this recipe, the green beans are fried, just like the cod, but you can substitute sautéed, steamed, or boiled green beans for the tempura green beans.

Yield: 4 thin rolls or 24 pieces

Prep time: 40 minutes

Cook time: 20 minutes

Ingredients:

- 1 (½ pound) cod fillet, cut into
- 2½-inch-thick sticks
- 2 tablespoons cornstarch
- Vegetable oil, for frying
- Tempura Batter
- 16 green beans, trimmed
- 2 whole nori sheets, halved

- 2 cups Sushi Rice
- Soy sauce (gluten-free if necessary)

Directions:

1. Lay the cod on paper towels and blot dry. Dust the cod lightly with the cornstarch.
2. In a deep pan, heat 2 inches of vegetable oil over medium-low heat until it shimmers. Dip the cod into the batter, then fry for 4 minutes, occasionally flipping, until golden. Transfer to a wire rack to drain.
3. Dip the green beans into the batter, then fry for 2 to 3 minutes, flipping occasionally. Transfer to a wire rack to drain.
4. Put the makisu on a work surface. Place one piece of nori on it, shiny-side down. Spread ½ cup of sushi rice evenly over the nori, leaving a ½-inch border on the far side.
5. Across the middle of the rice, place one-quarter of the cod tempura and 4 green beans.
6. Pick up the edge of the makisu and nori closest to you, attach the near edge of rice to the far edge of

the rice, and roll-up. Let it sit, seam-side down, for a few minutes. Make three more rolls with the remaining nori, rice, and filling.

7. Cut each sushi roll into 6 pieces and serve with soy sauce.

4.16 Crab Salad Roll

GLUTEN-FREE, NUT-FREE, PESCATARIAN

Crabmeat dressed with mayonnaise goes really well with lettuce and sushi rice. There are a couple of substitutions you can use with this recipe: imitation crabmeat for real crabmeat and regular mayonnaise for the wasabi mayonnaise sauce. In addition, lettuce can be used instead of nori. In that case, it is hard to keep a good sushi shape, so place the lettuce-wrapped sushi seam-side down on a plate.

Yield: 4 thin rolls or 24 pieces

Prep time: 45 minutes

Cook time: 7 minutes

Ingredients:

- 1 (4¼-ounce) can crabmeat, drained
- 3 tablespoons mayonnaise
- Salt
- Freshly ground black pepper
- 2 whole nori sheets, halved
- 2 cups Sushi Rice

- 4 tablespoons roasted sesame seeds
- 2 romaine lettuce leaves, halved lengthwise Wasabi Mayonnaise Sauce

Directions:

1. In a small bowl, stir together the crabmeat and mayonnaise. Season with salt and pepper.
2. Put the makisu on a work surface and place one piece of nori on it, shiny-side down. Spread ½ cup of rice evenly over the nori. Sprinkle with 1 tablespoon of sesame seeds. Put a piece of plastic wrap or parchment paper (about the same size as the makisu) on the rice and flip so the nori side is up.
3. Place one piece of lettuce on the nori and place 2 tablespoons of the crabmeat mixture across the middle of the lettuce.
4. Pick up the edge of the makisu and nori into a tight jelly roll. Let it sit, seam-side down, for a few minutes. Make three more rolls with the remaining nori, rice, sesame seeds, and filling.
5. Cut each sushi roll into 6 pieces and drizzle with the mayonnaise sauce.

4.17 Thai Shrimp Roll

GLUTEN-FREE, PESCATARIAN

Thai food uses many vegetables, seafood, and lots of flavorful spices. If you like spicy Thai food, spread chili sauce on the nori before rolling it up. This is a thin roll, so I recommend using medium-size shrimp because it is hard to roll a large shrimp properly.

Yield: 4 thin rolls or 24 pieces

Prep time: 50 minutes

Cook time: 5 minutes

Ingredients:

- 8 medium shrimp, deveined
- 2 whole nori sheets, halved
- 2 cups Sushi Rice
- ½ cup bean sprouts washed
- 8 cilantro sprigs, washed and trimmed
- ½ cup peanuts, crushed Peanut Sauce

Directions:

1. Fill a deep pan with water and bring it to a boil over high heat.
2. Skewer the shrimp from head to tail to prevent it from curling when cooked. Boil the shrimp over medium heat for 2 to 3 minutes, until it turns pink.
3. Place the makisu on a work surface and place one piece of nori on it, shiny-side down. Spread ½ cup of rice evenly over the nori. Put a piece of plastic wrap or parchment paper (about the same size as the makisu) on the rice and flip so the nori side is up.
4. Place 2 shrimp across the middle of the nori and arrange one quarter of the sprouts and 2 cilantro sprigs below the shrimp.
5. Pick up the edge of the makisu and nori it into a tight jelly roll. Let it sit, seam-side down, for a few minutes. Make three more rolls with the remaining nori, rice, and filling.
6. Cut each sushi roll into 6 pieces and serve sprinkled with peanuts and the peanut sauce drizzled on top.

4.18 Buttery Scallop Roll

GLUTEN-FREE, NUT-FREE, PESCATARIAN

Buttery soy sauce with scallops is a favorite flavor of the Japanese. In this recipe, the scallop is halved to make it easier to cook all the way through. There are three ways to confirm that scallops are cooked through: by color (they should be golden brown on both sides), by texture (the scallop should break apart a little along the edge), and by consistency (with a touch of a finger, scallops come apart easily).

Yield: 2 big rolls or 12 pieces

Prep time: 40 minutes

Cook time: 20 minutes

Ingredients:

- 2 tablespoons butter or margarine
- 12 scallops, halved horizontally
- 8 asparagus stalks, trimmed
- 2 tablespoons soy sauce (gluten-free if necessary)
- ½ cup fresh corn kernels

- 2 whole nori sheets, halved
- 2 cups Sushi Rice
- 4 tablespoons roasted sesame seeds

Directions:

1. In a skillet, melt 1 tablespoon of butter over medium heat. Add half the scallops and half the asparagus, and sauté for 5 minutes, flipping halfway through. Add 1 tablespoon of soy sauce and stir for 2 minutes. Transfer to a plate. Repeat with the remaining butter, scallops, asparagus, and soy sauce.
2. Add the corn to the empty skillet, and stir-fry over medium heat for about 5 minutes while scraping up the seasonings on the bottom of the skillet. Set aside.
3. Layout the makisu on a work surface and place one piece of nori on it, shiny-side down. Spread ½ cup of rice evenly over the nori. Sprinkle with 1 tablespoon of the sesame seeds. Put a piece of plastic wrap or parchment paper (about the same size as the makisu) on the rice and flip so the nori side is up.

4. Lay 2 asparagus stalks across the middle of the nori, and arrange 6 scallop pieces on the asparagus.
5. Pick up the edge of the makisu and nori into a tight jelly roll. Let it sit, seam-side down, for a few minutes. Make three more rolls with the remaining nori, rice, sesame seeds, and filling.
6. Cut each sushi roll into 6 pieces, top each piece with 1 teaspoon of the corn, and serve.

4.19 Fried Shrimp Roll

NUT-FREE, PESCATARIAN

This sushi has beautiful colors from the lettuce and egg and a crunchy texture from the fried shrimp. This roll has an eye-catching cross-section due to the layered shrimp, fried egg, lettuce, nori, and rice. In Japan, both fried and tempura shrimp are very popular and are frequently served as homemade dishes and at restaurants. The numerous steps may seem excessive, but it's worth it. This sushi is delicious!

Yield: 2 big rolls or 12 pieces

Prep time: 45 minutes

Cook time: 10 minutes

Ingredients:

- 1 teaspoon cornstarch
- 1 teaspoon water
- 2 eggs, beaten
- Nonstick cooking spray
- 4 large tail-on shrimp, deveined
- tablespoons all-purpose flour

- ½ cup bread crumbs
- Vegetable oil, for frying
- Whole nori sheets
- 2 cups Sushi Rice
- Romaine lettuce leaf halved lengthwise
- Tempura Batter Bits
- Soy Sauce, Mayonnaise Sauce

Directions:

1. In a small dish, whisk together the cornstarch and water. Mix in the beaten egg.
2. Heat an 8-inch nonstick skillet over medium-high heat and coat with cooking spray. Pour half of the egg mixture into the skillet and spread to make a thin layer. Cook over low heat for 3 minutes, flipping halfway through the cooking time. Make a second thin fried egg with the remaining egg mixture.
3. Make small cuts vertically on the shrimp belly, place belly-side down on a cutting board, and press the shrimp lightly to straighten. Bread the shrimp by coating them in the flour, then the egg, and then the bread crumbs.

4. In a deep pan, heat 2 inches of vegetable oil over medium heat until it shimmers. Fry the shrimp for 2 minutes, occasionally flipping, until golden. Transfer to a wire rack to drain.
5. Layout the makisu on a work surface and place one sheet of nori on top, shiny side down. Spread 1 cup of rice evenly over the nori. Put a piece of plastic wrap or parchment paper (about the same size as the makisu) on the rice and flip so the nori side is up.
6. Place a thin fried egg on the nori. Across the middle of the egg, place a piece of lettuce. On top of the lettuce, place 2 shrimp, tails sticking out from the nori.
7. Pick up the edge of the makisu and nori into a tight jelly roll. Let it sit, seam-side down, for 5 minutes at room temperature. Make another roll with the remaining nori, rice, and filling.
8. Cut each sushi roll into 6 pieces, sprinkle with the tempura batter bits, drizzle with the mayonnaise sauce, and serve.

COOKING TIP: The cornstarch keeps the thin fried egg from tearing. However, if the egg cooks too long, it can shatter.

4.20 Sweet Chili Shrimp Roll

GLUTEN-FREE, NUT-FREE, PESCATARIAN

Sweet chili sauce is a versatile sauce that can be easily transformed into other delicious sauces with a little ingenuity. A mixture of sweet chili, ketchup, and soy sauce is a great sauce for Chinese dishes, like sweet-and-sour pork. You can find sweet chili sauce at many Asian markets and on Amazon.

Yield: 4 thin rolls or 24 pieces

Prep time: 50 minutes

Cook time: 5 minutes

Ingredients:

- 8 medium shrimp, deveined
- 2 whole nori sheets, halved
- 2 cups Sushi Rice
- 4 tablespoons roasted sesame seeds
- 2 tablespoons sweet chili sauce
- ½ cup shredded red cabbage
- ½ cup bean sprouts washed
- Sweet Chili Mayonnaise Sauce

Directions:

1. Fill a deep pan with water and bring it to a boil over high heat.
2. Skewer the shrimp from head to tail to prevent it from curling when cooked—Boil the shrimp over medium heat for 2 to 3 minutes, or until it, turns pink.
3. Put the makisu on a work surface and place one piece of nori on it, shiny-side down. Spread ½ cup of rice evenly over the nori and sprinkle 1 tablespoon of the sesame seeds on top. Put a piece of plastic wrap or parchment paper (about the same size as the makisu) on the rice and flip so the nori side is up.
4. Spread ½ tablespoon of chili sauce in a line across the middle of the nori. Place 2 shrimp on the sauce. Add one-quarter of the cabbage and one-quarter of the sprouts below the shrimp.
5. Pick up the edge of the makisu and nori into a tight jelly roll. Let it sit, seam-side down, for a few minutes. Make three more rolls with the remaining nori, rice, sesame seeds, and filling.

Cut each sushi roll into 6 pieces and drizzle with chili mayonnaise.

4.21 Negitoro Tempura Roll

GLUTEN-FREE, NUT-FREE, PESCATARIAN

When I first saw a fried sushi roll in my college cafeteria in the United States, I was so surprised and at a loss for words because I had never seen sushi cooked that way. It tasted great, so now I sometimes fry simple sushi rolls that contain one or two fillings. To make well-shaped fried rolls, hold the roll tightly as you're rolling. If the roll is loose, it can easily fall apart when it is dipped in the tempura batter.

Yield: 4 thin rolls or 24 pieces

Prep time: 50 minutes

Cook time: 10 minutes

Ingredients:

- 4 ounces sashimi-grade tuna, finely minced
- 1 tablespoon soy sauce (gluten-free if necessary)
- 1 scallion, both white and green parts, chopped
- 2 whole nori sheets, halved
- 2 cups Sushi Rice
- Vegetable oil, for frying

- Tempura Batter
- Tempura Dashi Sauce

Directions:

1. In a mixing bowl, stir together the tuna, soy sauce, and scallion.
2. Layout the makisu on a work surface and place one piece of nori on it, shiny-side down. Spread ½ cup of rice evenly over the nori, leaving a ½-inch border on the far side.
3. Spread 2 tablespoons of the tuna mixture in a line across the middle of the rice.
4. Pick up the edge of the makisu and nori closest to you, attach the near edge of rice to the far side of the rice, and roll-up. Let it sit, seam-side down, until the nori sticks firmly, for a few minutes. Make three more rolls with the remaining nori, rice, and filling.
5. In a deep pan, heat 2 inches of vegetable oil over medium heat until it shimmers. Dip the rolls in the batter, then fry until golden, about 2 to 3 minutes.

Transfer to a wire rack to drain. Repeat with the remaining rolls.

6. Cut the sushi roll into 6 pieces and serve with a dish of dashi sauce.

4.22 Fried Avocado Roll

NUT-FREE, PESCATARIAN

It seems that almost all sushi rolls around the world contain avocado. This roll contains fried avocado, sashimi tuna, and smoked salmon—a great combination of good fat and protein. The keys to cooking perfect fried avocado are to use avocado before it is ripe and to batter it properly. When the bread crumbs don't stick well to the avocado, dip the breaded avocado into the egg again and then press it into the bread crumbs.

Yield: 2 big rolls or 12 pieces

Prep time: 35 minutes

Cook time: 10 minutes

Ingredients:

- 1 avocado, cut lengthwise into 8 equal pieces
- 3 tablespoons all-purpose flour
- 1 egg, beaten
- ¾ cup bread crumbs
- Vegetable oil, for frying

- 2 whole nori sheets
- 2 cups Sushi Rice
- 4 tablespoons roasted sesame seeds
- 4 ounces sashimi-grade tuna, cut
- 4 ounces sliced smoked salmon
- Sweet Eel Sauce

Directions:

1. Coat the avocado pieces in the flour, then the beaten egg, and then the bread crumbs.
2. In a deep pan, heat 2 inches of vegetable oil over medium heat until it shimmers. Add the avocado pieces and fry for 2 to 3 minutes, occasionally flipping, until golden. Transfer to a wire rack to drain.
3. Layout the makisu on a work surface and place one sheet of nori on it, shiny-side down. Spread 1 cup of rice evenly over the nori. Sprinkle the rice with 2 tablespoons of sesame seeds. Put a piece

   of plastic wrap or parchment paper (about the same size as the makisu) on the rice and flip so the nori side is up.

4. Lay 4 pieces of the avocado across the middle of the nori, and arrange half of the tuna below the avocado.
5. Pick up the edge of the makisu and nori into a tight jelly roll. Remove the wrap and makisu, place the roll seam-side down, and arrange half of the smoked salmon slices next to each other lengthwise over the roll. Cover the roll with the plastic wrap and hold it tightly to make the salmon stick to the roll firmly. Let it sit for 5 minutes at room temperature. Make another roll with the remaining nori, rice, sesame seeds, filling, and topping.
6. Cut each sushi roll into 6 pieces, drizzle with the sauce, and serve.

CLEANUP TIP: Do not drain the used oil down the sink. Instead, stuff paper towels into an empty can or jar for absorption, and pour the cooled oil into the container. Throw the can or jar into the regular garbage.

4.23 Spicy Salmon Roll

GLUTEN-FREE, NUT-FREE, PESCATARIAN

The spicy tuna roll may be the most famous roll globally, but the popularity of the spicy salmon roll is catching up. Eating this spicy salmon roll is going to be an eye-opening experience for you. Sashimi salmon, spicy mayonnaise, and sharp-flavored arugula are put together in one roll. On top, the roll is covered with sliced cucumber and garnished with a lemon zest that brings fresh taste and great balance.

Yield: 4 thin rolls or 24 pieces

Prep time: 45 minutes

Cook time: 12 minutes

Ingredients:

- 2 whole nori sheets, halved
- 2 cups Sushi Rice
- 2 tablespoons Spicy Mayonnaise Sauce
- 1 cup baby arugula
- 4 ounces sashimi-grade salmon, cut
- 3 baby cucumbers, very thinly sliced lengthwise

- Zest of 1 lemon

Directions:

1. Layout the makisu on a work surface and place one piece of nori on it, shiny-side down. Spread ½ cup of rice evenly over the nori. Put a piece of plastic wrap or parchment paper (about the same size as the makisu) on the rice and flip so the nori side is up.
2. Spread ½ tablespoon of the sauce in a line across the middle of the nori. Spread one-quarter of the arugula on top of the sauce, and lay 3 pieces of the salmon on the arugula.
3. Pick up the edge of the makisu and nori into a tight jelly roll. Remove the wrap and makisu, place the roll seam-side down, and arrange the cucumber slices lengthwise on a slight diagonal over the roll. Cover the roll with the plastic wrap and hold it tightly to make the cucumber stick to the roll firmly. Let it sit for a few minutes. Make three more rolls with the remaining nori, rice, and filling.
4. Cut each sushi roll into 6 pieces, sprinkle with lemon zest, and serve.

4.24 Egg Roll

GLUTEN-FREE, NUT-FREE, VEGETARIAN

This is a very delicious and good-looking sushi roll wrapped with a thin layer of fried egg instead of nori. Because the egg wrapper has a round shape and the fried egg doesn't stick to any other ingredients, use less rice than you would in a regular thin roll and serve the cut sushi pieces seam-side down on a plate. Egg-wrapped sushi is very popular among my non-Japanese friends. It is a great recipe to master!

Yield: 3 thin rolls or 12 pieces

Prep time: 35 minutes

Cook time: 10 minutes

Ingredients:

- 1 teaspoon cornstarch
- 1 teaspoon water
- 1 teaspoon soy sauce (gluten-free if necessary)
- 2 eggs, beaten
- Nonstick cooking spray

- 1 cup Sushi Rice
- 1½ baby cucumbers, cut
- ½ avocado cut lengthwise into 6 equal pieces

Directions:

1. In a small dish, whisk together the cornstarch and water. Mix in the soy sauce and the beaten eggs.
2. Heat an 8-inch nonstick skillet over medium-high heat and coat with cooking spray. Pour one-third of the egg mixture into the skillet and spread the egg over the surface of the skillet to make a thin layer. Cook over low heat for 3 minutes, flipping halfway through. Make two more thin fried eggs with the remaining egg mixture.
3. Layout the makisu on a work surface and place one egg on top. Spread ⅓ cup of rice evenly over half the egg. Press the rice lightly.
4. Place 2 pieces of cucumber and 2 pieces of avocado on the rice.
5. Pick up the edge of the makisu and nori into a tight jelly roll. Let it sit, seam-side down, for a few minutes.

Make two more rolls with the remaining eggs, rice, and filling.

6. Cut each sushi roll into 4 pieces and serve.

COOKING TIP: Wrap the makisu with pieces of paper towel, parchment paper, or plastic wrap before placing the fried egg on top. This keeps the makisu from getting oil stains.

4.25 Salmon Teriyaki Roll

GLUTEN-FREE, NUT-FREE, PESCATARIAN

Do you struggle with cooking salmon all the way through? In this recipe, I introduce you to seared sashimi salmon, where it doesn't matter if the inside of the salmon is uncooked. Salmon sashimi has an incredibly soft texture because of its high-fat content. In comparison, tuna sashimi tends to get hard quickly when it's cooked. While you're cooking the salmon, treat it gently, or it falls apart easily.

Yield: 4 thin rolls or 24 pieces

Prep time: 40 minutes

Cook time: 10 minutes

Ingredients:

- 4 ounces sashimi-grade salmon, cut
- ¼ cup Sweet Eel Sauce
- 2 whole nori sheets, halved
- 2 cups Sushi Rice
- 4 tablespoons roasted sesame seeds
- 8 parsley sprigs, trimmed

- Wasabi Mayonnaise Sauce
- 4 scallions, both white and green parts, chopped

Directions:

1. In a dry nonstick skillet, cook the salmon over medium-low heat for 4 minutes, flipping occasionally. Add the eel sauce and cook for 2 minutes more, frequently flipping to coat the salmon.
2. Layout the makisu and place one piece of nori on top, shiny side down. Spread ½ cup of rice evenly over the nori. Spread 1 tablespoon of sesame seeds on the rice. Put a piece of plastic wrap or parchment paper (about the same size as the makisu) on the rice and flip so the nori side is up.
3. Arrange 3 pieces of salmon and 2 parsley sprigs across the middle of the nori.
4. Pick up the edge of the makisu and nori into a tight jelly roll. Let it sit, seam-side down, for a few minutes. Make three more rolls with the remaining nori, rice, sesame seeds, and filling.
5. Cut each sushi roll into 6 pieces, drizzle with the sauce, sprinkle with the scallions, and serve.

4.26 Spicy Crab and Mango Roll

GLUTEN-FREE, NUT-FREE, PESCATARIAN

Mango brings out the flavor of seafood very well. If you haven't eaten these two things together, try this roll. It has a wonderfully spicy and fresh taste with a touch of sweetness from the mango. You can use a 4¼-ounce can of lump crabmeat for this recipe if you prefer. Just be sure to drain before seasoning. You can also use imitation crab or any cooked seafood instead of crab.

Yield: 4 thin rolls or 24 pieces

Prep time: 45 minutes

Cook time: 10 minutes

Ingredients:

- 4 ounces cooked crabmeat, coarsely chopped
- 1 teaspoon sweet chili sauce salt
- Freshly ground black pepper
- Juice of ½ lemon
- 2 whole nori sheets, halved
- 2 cups Sushi Rice

- ½ avocado, cut
- 1 cup Spicy Mango Sauce

1. In a bowl, stir together the crabmeat, the sweet chili sauce, a pinch of salt and pepper, and the lemon juice.
2. Layout the makisu on a work surface and place one piece of nori on it, shiny-side down. Spread ½ cup of rice evenly over the nori. Put a piece of plastic wrap or parchment paper (about the same size as the makisu) on the rice and flip so the nori side is up.
3. Spread 2 tablespoons of the crab mixture in a line across the middle of the nori. Place 2 or 3 slices of avocado on top of the crab mixture.
4. Pick up the edge of the makisu and nori into a tight jelly roll. Make three more rolls with the remaining nori, rice, and filling.
5. Cut each sushi roll into 6 pieces, top with the mango sauce, and serve.

4.27 Spicy Fried Mozzarella Roll

NUT-FREE, VEGETARIAN

The main ingredient of this roll is fried mozzarella cheese sticks, which everybody loves. If you don't like spicy food, substitute ketchup for the Pico de Gallo and the spicy mayonnaise sauce. In fact, the combination of rice and ketchup is very popular in Japan. It is delicious!

Yield: 2 big rolls or 12 pieces

Prep time: 35 minutes

Cook time: 2 minutes

Ingredients:

- 3 mozzarella cheese sticks, halved
- 2 tablespoons all-purpose flour
- 1 egg, beaten
- ½ cup bread crumbs
- Vegetable oil, for frying
- 2 whole nori sheets
- 2 cups Sushi Rice
- 4 tablespoons roasted sesame seeds

- 1 romaine lettuce leaf, halved lengthwise
- ½ cup Pico de Gallo
- Spicy Mayonnaise Sauce

Directions:

1. Coat the mozzarella sticks in flour, then egg, and then bread crumbs.

2. In a deep pan, heat 2 inches of vegetable oil over medium heat until it shimmers. Fry the mozzarella, flipping occasionally, until golden, about 30 to 60 seconds. Transfer to a wire rack to drain.

3. Layout the makisu on a work surface and place one piece of nori on top, shiny side down. Spread 1 cup of sushi rice evenly over the nori. Spread 2 tablespoons of the sesame seeds on the rice. Put a piece of plastic wrap or parchment paper (about the same size as the makisu) on the rice and flip so the nori side is up.

4. Place a piece of lettuce across the middle of the nori. Place 3 pieces of the fried mozzarella on the

lettuce, and spread ¼ cup of the Pico de Gallo in a line below the mozzarella.

5. Pick up the edge of the makisu and nori into a tight jelly roll. Let it sit for 5 minutes at room temperature. Make another roll with the remaining nori, rice, sesame seeds, and filling.
6. Cut each sushi roll into 6 pieces, drizzle with mayonnaise sauce, and serve.

4.28 Asparagus Roll

GLUTEN-FREE, NUT-FREE, VEGETARIAN

This roll combines popular Japanese breakfast ingredients into one roll. It has a great balance of nutrients from the egg, asparagus, sesame seeds, and miso. This roll is a great dish for parties because it is gluten-free, vegetarian, and delicious, so most people can enjoy it. Frying is one of the best ways to cook asparagus. It makes for a good, tender texture in a short amount of time.

Yield: 4 thin rolls or 24 pieces

Prep time: 45 minutes

Cook time: 5 minutes

Ingredients:

- Vegetable oil, for frying
- 8 asparagus stalks, trimmed and washed
- Tempura Batter
- 2 whole nori sheets, halved
- 2 cups Sushi Rice
- 4 tablespoons roasted sesame seeds

- Japanese Egg Omelet quartered lengthwise and each quarter halved crosswise
- Miso Sesame Sauce

Directions:

1. In a deep pan, heat 2 inches of vegetable oil over medium-low heat until it shimmers. Dip the asparagus into the batter, then fry for 2 minutes, occasionally flipping, until golden. Transfer to a wire rack to drain.
2. Layout the makisu on a work surface and place one piece of nori on top, shiny side down. Spread ½ cup of rice evenly over the nori. Sprinkle 1 tablespoon of the sesame seeds over the rice. Place a piece of plastic wrap or parchment paper (about the same size as the makisu) on the rice and flip so the nori side is up.
3. Place 2 pieces of asparagus across the middle of the nori and arrange 1 or 2 omelet sticks below the asparagus.
4. Pick up the edge of the makisu and nori into a tight jelly roll. Let it sit, seam-side down, for 2 minutes. Make

three more rolls with the remaining nori, rice, sesame seeds, and filling.

5. Cut each sushi roll into 6 pieces, drizzle the sauce on top, and serve.

4.29 Zucchini Roll

NUT-FREE, VEGETARIAN

With this recipe, I use black pepper for seasoning, but you can substitute sweet chili sauce if you prefer. The key to frying zucchini is to flour it well when breading it. If it is not coated well, the bread crumbs won't stick.

Yield: 4 thin rolls or 24 pieces

Prep time: 50 minutes

Cook time: 15 minutes

Ingredients:

- 1 zucchini, cut into
- ½-inch-thick sticks
- 3 tablespoons all-purpose flour
- 1 egg, beaten
- ¾ cup bread crumbs
- Vegetable oil, for frying
- 2 whole nori sheets, halved
- 2 cups Sushi Rice

- ¾ (8-ounce) package cream cheese, cut into ½-inch-thick sticks
- 1 avocado, cut
- Freshly ground black pepper

Directions:

1. Bread the zucchini by rolling it in the flour, then the egg, and then the bread crumbs.
2. In a deep pan, heat 2 inches of vegetable oil over medium heat until it shimmers. Fry the zucchini for 2 to 3 minutes, in batches, if necessary, until golden. Transfer to a wire rack to drain.
3. Layout the makisu on a work surface and place one piece of nori on top, shiny side down. Spread ½ cup of rice evenly over the nori. Put a piece of plastic wrap or parchment paper (about the same size as the makisu) on the rice and flip so the nori side is up.
4. Arrange 2 or 3 pieces of the zucchini across the middle of the nori. Add 1 or 2 pieces of the cream cheese below the zucchini.

5. Pick up the edge of the makisu and nori into a tight jelly roll. Remove the wrap and makisu, place the roll seam-side down, and arrange one-quarter of the avocado slices next to one another lengthwise over the roll. Cover the roll with the plastic wrap and hold it tightly to make the avocado stick to the roll firmly. Let it sit for 5 minutes at room temperature. Make three more rolls with the remaining nori, rice, filling, and topping.

Cut each sushi roll into 6 pieces, sprinkle with the black pepper, and serve.

4.30 Sweet Potato Tempura Roll

GLUTEN-FREE, NUT-FREE, VEGAN

Sweet potato tempura has never been the main dish in Japan, but it is a very popular tempura ingredient. To make sure that the potato tempura is done, poke it with a toothpick, and when the toothpick slides all the way easily through, it is done. If not, fry for one more minute.

Yield: 2 big rolls or 12 pieces

Prep time: 30 minutes

Cook time: 15 minutes

Ingredients:

- Vegetable oil, for frying
- ½ medium sweet potato, peeled and cut into ½-inch-thick sticks
- Tempura Batter
- 4 shiitake mushrooms, stemmed and halved
- 2 whole nori sheets
- 2 cups Sushi Rice
- 4 tablespoons roasted sesame seeds
- Tempura Dashi Sauce

Directions:

1. In a deep pan, heat 2 inches of vegetable oil over medium-low heat until it shimmers. Dip the sweet potato sticks into the batter, then fry about 4 pieces at a time for 3 minutes, occasionally flipping, until golden. Transfer to a wire rack to drain.

2. Dip the mushrooms into the batter, then fry for 1 to 2 minutes, flipping occasionally. Transfer to a wire rack to drain.

3. Layout the makisu on a work surface and place one sheet of nori on top, shiny side down. Spread 1 cup of sushi rice evenly over the nori. Sprinkle the rice with 2 tablespoons of the sesame seeds. Put a piece of plastic wrap or parchment paper (about the same size as the makisu) on the rice and flip so the nori side is up.

4. Arrange half of the sweet potato tempura in a line across the middle of the nori, and place 4 pieces of the shiitake mushrooms below the sweet potatoes.

5. Pick up the edge of the makisu and nori into a tight jelly roll. Let it sit, seam-side down, for 5 minutes at

room temperature. Make another roll with the remaining nori, rice, sesame seeds, and filling.

6. Cut each sushi roll into 6 pieces and serve with a dish of dashi sauce.

4.31 Quinoa Salad Roll

GLUTEN-FREE, VEGAN

This creative sushi roll uses quinoa instead of rice. Unlike rice, cooked quinoa is not sticky, so make sure to press it well when it is spread on the nori and to roll nori-side out. Using quinoa has an advantage, as it doesn't dry out easily in the refrigerator like sushi rice. Therefore, you can make this roll ahead of time and keep it in the refrigerator, just like a quinoa salad!

Yield: 2 big rolls or 12 pieces

Prep time: 25 minutes

Cook time: 10 minutes

Ingredients:

- 2 whole nori sheets
- 1 cup cooked quinoa
- ½ cup arugula
- ½ yellow bell pepper, sliced
- 1 medium tomato, seeded and sliced
- ½ avocado
- Almond Sauce

Directions:

1. Layout the makisu on a work surface and place one sheet of nori on it, shiny-side down. Spread ½ cup of the quinoa evenly over the nori, leaving a 2-inch border on the far side.

2. Place ¼ cup of arugula in a line across the middle of the quinoa. Place half of the bell pepper, half of the tomato, and half of the avocado on the arugula.

3. Pick up the edge of the makisu and nori into a jelly roll. Let it sit for 5 minutes at room temperature. Make another roll with the remaining nori, quinoa, and filling.

4. Cut each sushi roll into 6 pieces, drizzle with almond sauce, and serve.

4.32 Rainbow Veggie Roll

GLUTEN-FREE, NUT-FREE, VEGAN

This roll is a great lunch to eat on the go and becomes even easier on your schedule if you make it the night before. You can store this overnight in the refrigerator, but be sure to drizzle the avocado with juice from half a lemon, so it does not turn brown.

Yield: 2 big rolls or 12 pieces

Prep time: 30 minutes, plus 20 minutes to marinate

Cook time: 5 minutes

Ingredients:

- 1 tablespoon toasted sesame oil
- ½ yellow bell pepper, sliced
- ½ cup Pickling Liquid
- 2 whole nori sheets
- 2 cups Sushi Rice
- 4 tablespoons roasted sesame seeds
- 1 romaine lettuce leaf, halved lengthwise
- 1 baby cucumber, cut

- ½ cup shredded red cabbage
- 1 avocado, cut
- Finely ground Himalayan pink salt

Directions:

1. In a skillet, heat the sesame oil over medium heat until it shimmers. Add the bell pepper and cook for 5 minutes. In a bowl, stir together the bell pepper and the pickling liquid. Let it sit for 20 minutes at room temperature.
2. Lay out the makisu on a work surface and place one sheet of nori on top, shiny side down. Spread 1 cup of sushi rice evenly over the nori. Sprinkle 2 tablespoons of the sesame seeds on top of the rice. Put a piece of plastic wrap or parchment paper (about the same size as the makisu) on the rice and flip so the nori side is up.
3. Lay a piece of the lettuce across the middle of the nori. Place 2 pieces of the cucumber, ¼ cup of the cabbage, and half of the pickled bell pepper on the lettuce.

4. Pick up the edge of the makisu and nori into a tight jelly roll. Remove the wrap and makisu, place the roll seam-side down, and arrange half of the avocado slices side by side lengthwise over the roll. Cover the roll with the wrap, and hold tightly to make the avocado stick to the roll firmly. Let it sit for 5 minutes at room temperature. Make another roll with the remaining nori, rice, sesame seeds, filling, and topping.
5. Cut each sushi roll into 6 pieces, sprinkle with salt, and serve.

4.33 Chicken Katsu Roll

NUT-FREE

Chicken Katsu (fried chicken breast) is a staple dish in Japan. Katsu means "win" in Japanese, so sometimes people eat this before an exam or a game for good luck.

Yield: 4 thin rolls or 24 pieces

Prep time: 45 minutes

Cook time: 10 minutes

Ingredients:

- 6 ounces chicken breast, cut into ½-inch-wide strips
- Salt
- Freshly ground black pepper
- 2 tablespoons all-purpose flour
- 1 egg, beaten
- ½ cup bread crumbs
- Vegetable oil, for frying
- 2 whole nori sheets, halved
- 2 cups Sushi Rice

- 4 tablespoons roasted sesame seeds
- 1 cup shredded cabbage
- Sweet Eel Sauce

Directions:

1. Season the chicken with salt and pepper.
2. Coat the chicken in the flour, then the egg, and then the bread crumbs.
3. In a deep pan, heat 2 inches of vegetable oil over medium heat until it shimmers. Fry the chicken for about 4 minutes, until golden, flipping occasionally. Transfer to a wire rack to drain.
4. Lay out the makisu on a work surface and place one piece of nori on top, shiny side down. Spread ½ cup of rice evenly over the nori. Sprinkle with 1 tablespoon of sesame seeds. Place a piece of plastic wrap or parchment paper (about the same size as the makisu) on the rice and flip so the nori side is up.

   Place one-quarter of the chicken across the middle of the nori, and place ¼ cup of the cabbage below the chicken.

5. Pick up the edge of the makisu and nori into a tight jelly roll. Let it sit, seam-side down, for a few minutes. Make three more rolls with the remaining nori, rice, sesame seeds, and filling.
6. Cut each sushi roll into 6 pieces, drizzle with the sauce, and serve.

SUBSTITUTION TIP: You can substitute lettuce for cabbage if you prefer.

4.34 Chicken Sausage Roll

GLUTEN-FREE, NUT-FREE, KID FRIENDLY

This is the best sushi roll for kids—chicken sausage rolled with rice wrapped in a slightly sweet fried egg wrapper. You can substitute any kind of sausage you like. To fancy up this roll, serve with marinara sauce.

Yield: 3 thin rolls or 12 pieces

Prep time: 30 minutes

Cook time: 15 minutes

Ingredients:

- 3 chicken sausages
- 1 teaspoon cornstarch
- 1 teaspoon water1 teaspoon sugar
- 2 eggs, beaten
- Nonstick cooking spray
- 1 cup Sushi Rice Ketchup

Directions:

1. Cook the chicken sausages according to the package directions and set aside to cool.

2. In a small dish, whisk together the cornstarch and water. Mix in the sugar and the beaten eggs. Heat an 8-inch nonstick skillet over medium-high heat and coat with cooking spray. Pour one-third of the egg mixture into the skillet and spread the egg all over the surface of the skillet to make a thin layer. Cook over low heat for 3 minutes, gently flipping halfway through the cooking time with a rubber spatula. Make two more thin fried eggs with the remaining egg mixture.

3. Lay out the makisu on a work surface and place one piece of egg on top. Spread ⅓ cup of the rice evenly across half of the egg, and press the rice lightly.

4. Lay 1 sausage across the middle of the rice. Pick up the edge of the makisu and nori into a tight jelly roll. Let it sit, seam-side down, for 2 minutes. Make two more rolls with the remaining egg, rice, and sausage.

5. Cut each sushi roll into 4 pieces, top with a dash of ketchup, and serve.

COOKING TIP: Wrap the makisu with pieces of paper towel, parchment paper, or plastic before placing the fried egg on top to keep the makisu from getting stained.

4.35 Asparagus and Bacon Roll

GLUTEN-FREE, NUT-FREE

Asparagus and bacon are made for each other. In this recipe, turkey bacon is used, but you can use any kind of bacon you like. Use soy bacon to make this roll vegetarian. Bacon is the perfect length for sushi rolls, so there is no need to cut. However, when you roll, you should fold the edge of the bacon back into the roll because the roll doesn't close when the bacon sticks out.

Yield: 4 thin rolls or 24 pieces

Prep time: 40 minutes

Cook time: 20 minutes

Ingredients:

- 8 turkey bacon slices
- 8 asparagus stalks, trimmed
- 1 tablespoon butter or margarine
- 2 eggs, beaten
- 2 whole nori sheets, halved
- 2 cups Sushi Rice
- 4 tablespoons roasted sesame seeds

Directions:

1. In a dry nonstick skillet, cook the bacon. Transfer to a plate lined with paper towels to drain.
2. In the same skillet, cook the asparagus for 5 minutes, occasionally flipping, until softened slightly. Transfer to a plate.
3. In the skillet, melt the butter. Pour in the beaten egg and cook over medium heat for about 1 minute, moving a spatula across the bottom and sides of the skillet to make small curds. Remove from the heat and set aside.
4. Lay out the makisu on a work surface and place one piece of nori on it, shiny-side down. Spread ½ cup of rice evenly over the nori. Sprinkle the rice with 1 tablespoon of the sesame seeds. Put a piece of plastic wrap or parchment paper (about the same size as the makisu) on the rice and flip so the nori side is up.

   Lay one piece of bacon across the middle of the nori. On top of the bacon, layer 2 asparagus stalks and another piece of bacon.

5. Pick up the edge of makisu and nori closest to you, and roll into a tight jelly roll. Let it sit, seam-side down, for 2 minutes. Make three more rolls with the remaining nori, rice, sesame seeds, and filling.

6. Cut each sushi roll into 6 pieces, top with the cooked egg, and serve.

4.36 Taco Sushi Roll

GLUTEN-FREE, NUT-FREE

This roll includes traditional taco ingredients - meat, lettuce, cheese, and Pico de Gallo - wrapped just like a burrito. All of the ingredients are crumbled, so be sure to hold them properly with your fingers when you roll-up. For the ground beef, it is best to choose 80 to 90 percent lean beef. If low-fat meat is used, the roll may have a dry texture.

Yield: 2 big rolls or 4 pieces

Prep time: 25 minutes

Cook time: 10 minutes

Ingredients:

- 1 tablespoon vegetable oil
- 4 ounces ground beef
- ½ teaspoon onion powder
- ½ teaspoon ground cumin
- ½ teaspoon chili powder
- ½ teaspoon garlic powder

- ½ tablespoon ketchup
- Salt
- Freshly ground black pepper
- 2 whole nori sheets
- 2 cups Sushi Rice
- ½ cup shredded lettuce
- ½ cup Pico de Gallo
- ½ cup shredded cheddar cheese

Directions:

1. In a skillet, heat the vegetable oil over medium heat until it shimmers. Add the beef and cook, breaking it up with a spatula, until it is browned and no longer pink, about 5 minutes. Drain the excess fat, if any. Season with onion powder, ground cumin, chili powder, garlic powder, ketchup, salt, and pepper. Cook, stirring, for 2 minutes.
2. Put the makisu on a work surface. Place one sheet of nori on it, shiny side down, with the longer side closest to you. Using a wet rice paddle, spread 1 cup of sushi

rice evenly over the nori. Leave a 1-inch border on the far side of the nori.

3. Arrange ¼ cup of the beef in a line across the middle of the rice, and lay ¼ cup of the lettuce, ¼ cup of Pico de Gallo, and ¼ cup of the cheese below the beef.

4. Pick up the edge of the makisu and nori closest to you, and keep the filling in place with your fingers. Attach the near edge of the rice to the far edge of the rice and roll-up. Hold the roll tightly to form a good shape. Let it sit, seam-side down, for about 5 minutes at room temperature. Make another roll with the remaining nori, rice, and filling.

5. Wrap the roll with a piece of parchment paper. To serve, halve crosswise at an angle.

SUBSTITUTION TIP: You can add avocado or guacamole to the roll as a filling. In that case, reduce the other filling ingredients by half, so the roll will close well.

4.37 Korean-Inspired Beef Roll

GLUTEN-FREE, NUT-FREE

This sushi roll has a delicious Korean flavor from the beef and seasoned sprouts. It is a very flavorful dish! In this recipe, the beef is seasoned with salt and black pepper and sautéed with minced garlic, but barbecue sauce can be used for seasoning if you prefer.

Yield: 2 big rolls or 12 pieces

Prep time: 25 minutes

Cook time: 10 minutes

Ingredients:

- 4 ounces sirloin steak, chuck steak, or rib-eye steak, cut into ½-inch-thick strips
- Pinch salt, plus 1 teaspoon
- Freshly ground black pepper
- 1 tablespoon vegetable oil
- 2 garlic cloves, minced or grated, divided
- 1 cup bean sprouts, washed
- 1 tablespoon roasted sesame seeds

- 1 tablespoon toasted sesame oil
- 1 teaspoon soy sauce (gluten-free if necessary)
- 1 teaspoon sugar
- 2 whole nori sheets
- 2 cups Sushi Rice
- 2 scallions, both white and green parts, chopped Wasabi Mayonnaise Sauce

Directions:

1. Season the steak with a pinch of salt and black pepper. In a skillet, heat the oil and half of the garlic over medium heat until the garlic starts browning. Cook the beef for 7 to 8 minutes, occasionally flipping, until it browns completely.

2. Microwave the sprouts for 60 to 90 seconds, until tender. Once they're cool enough to handle, squeeze excess water out by hand. In a bowl, stir together the sprouts, the other half of the garlic, sesame seeds, sesame oil, soy sauce, sugar, and 1 teaspoon of salt. Lay out the makisu on a work surface and place one sheet of nori on top, shiny side down. Spread 1 cup of rice evenly over the nori, leaving a 1-inch border on the far side of the nori.

3. Lay half of the steak across the middle of the rice. Arrange half of the sprouts below the beef.

4. Pick up the edge of the makisu and nori, attach the near edge of the rice to the rice on the far side, and roll-up. Let it sit, seam-side down, for about 5 minutes at room temperature. Make another roll with the remaining nori, rice, and filling.

5. Cut each sushi roll into 6 pieces, sprinkle with scallions, drizzle with the mayonnaise sauce, and serve.

4.38 Sweet-and-Sour Pork Roll

GLUTEN-FREE, NUT-FREE

The Chinese dish sweet-and-sour pork is a very popular homemade food in Japan. The fruity pineapple tastes great in a roll! In fact, pineapple contains enzymes that break up proteins, which allows our bodies to digest the meat better. It is important for optimal health benefits that the pineapple not be cooked over 140°F. I use Spam to make this recipe easier and tastier. When you bite into this roll, you will be hit with delicious flavors.

Yield: 2 big rolls or 12 pieces

Prep time: 25 minutes

Cook time: 5 minutes

Ingredients:

- 1 tablespoon vegetable oil
- ½ (12-ounce) can Spam, diced
- ¼ onion, sliced
- ¼ cup Sweet-and-Sour Sauce, plus more for dressing the roll

- 2 whole nori sheets
- 2 cups Sushi Rice
- ½ cup chopped pineapple
- 2 scallions, both white and green parts, chopped

Directions:

1. In a skillet, heat the vegetable oil over medium heat until it shimmers. Add the Spam and the onion, and cook for 3 minutes. Add the sweet-and-sour sauce and stir-fry for 2 minutes, until the Spam and onion are well coated, then remove from the heat.
2. Lay out the makisu on a work surface and place one sheet of nori on top, shiny side down. Spread 1 cup of rice evenly over the nori. Put a piece of plastic wrap or parchment paper (about the same size as the makisu) on the rice and flip so the nori side is up.
3. Place half of the cooked meat mixture in a line across the middle of the nori, and lay ¼ cup of the pineapple below the meat.

4. Pick up the edge of the makisu and nori into a tight jelly roll. Let it sit, seam-side down, for about 5 minutes at room temperature.

Make another roll with the remaining nori, rice, and filling.

5. Cut each sushi roll into 6 pieces, sprinkle with the scallions, drizzle with the sauce, and serve.

4.39 Ginger Chicken Roll

GLUTEN-FREE, NUT-FREE

This is a typical homemade Japanese food. It is an incredibly delicious and flavorful dish. Pork is usually used in the traditional recipe, but I use chicken thigh because it is delicious and stays tender after getting cold. The cooked ginger chicken can be stored in the refrigerator for up to 4 days, so you can make it ahead of time and just microwave it with a cover for about 30 seconds when you're ready to make the roll.

Yield: 2 big rolls or 12 pieces

Prep time: 30 minutes, plus 15 minutes to marinate

Cook time: 10 minutes

Ingredients:

- 6 ounces boneless, skinless chicken thighs, cut into ½-inch-wide strips
- 2 teaspoons peeled, grated fresh ginger
- 2 tablespoons soy sauce (gluten-free if necessary)
- 2 tablespoons cooking sake

- 1 tablespoon mirin
- 1 tablespoon toasted sesame oil
- 2 whole nori sheets
- 2 cups Sushi Rice
- 4 tablespoons roasted sesame seeds
- ¼ onion, thinly sliced
- ½ cup shredded red cabbage
- 2 scallions, both white and green parts, chopped Mayonnaise

Directions:

1. In a large bowl, combine the chicken, ginger, soy sauce, cooking sake, and mirin. Stir until the chicken is coated. Refrigerate to marinate for at least 15 minutes.
2. In a skillet, heat the sesame oil over medium heat until it shimmers. Add the chicken with the marinade and cook for 7 minutes, stirring continuously, until the chicken is cooked through.
3. Lay out the makisu on a work surface and place one sheet of nori on top, shiny side down. Spread 1 cup

of rice evenly over the nori. Sprinkle 2 tablespoons of sesame seeds on top. Put a piece of plastic wrap or parchment paper (about the same size as the makisu) on the rice and flip so the nori side is up.

4. Place half of the chicken in a line across the middle of the nori, and lay half of the onion and ¼ cup of the red cabbage below the chicken.

5. Pick up the edge of the makisu and nori into a tight jelly roll. Let it sit, seam-side down, for about 5 minutes at room temperature. Make another roll with the remaining nori, rice, sesame seeds, and filling. Cut each sushi roll into 6 pieces, sprinkle with the scallions, drizzle with the mayonnaise, and serve.

4.40 Sweet-and-Sour Pork Roll

GLUTEN-FREE, NUT-FREE

The Chinese dish sweet-and-sour pork is a very popular homemade food in Japan. The fruity pineapple tastes great in a roll! In fact, pineapple contains enzymes that break up proteins, which allows our bodies to digest the meat better. It is important for optimal health benefits that the pineapple not be cooked over 140°F. I use Spam to make this recipe easier and tastier. When you bite into this roll, you will be hit with delicious flavors.

Yield: 2 big rolls or 12 pieces

Prep time: 25 minutes

Cook time: 5 minutes

Ingredients:

- 1 tablespoon vegetable oil
- ½ (12-ounce) can Spam, diced
- ¼ onion, sliced
- ¼ cup Sweet-and-Sour Sauce, plus more for dressing the roll

- 2 whole nori sheets
- 2 cups Sushi Rice
- ½ cup chopped pineapple
- 2 scallions, both white and green parts, chopped

Directions:

1. In a skillet, heat the vegetable oil over medium heat until it shimmers. Add the Spam and the onion, and cook for 3 minutes. Add the sweet-and-sour sauce and stir-fry for 2 minutes, until the Spam and onion are well coated, then remove from the heat.
2. Lay out the makisu on a work surface and place one sheet of nori on top, shiny side down. Spread 1 cup of rice evenly over the nori. Put a piece of plastic wrap or parchment paper (about the same size as the makisu) on the rice and flip so the nori side is up.
3. Place half of the cooked meat mixture in a line across the middle of the nori, and lay ¼ cup of the pineapple below the meat.

4. Pick up the edge of the makisu and nori into a tight jelly roll. Let it sit, seam-side down, for about 5 minutes at room temperature.

   Make another roll with the remaining nori, rice, and filling.

Cut each sushi roll into 6 pieces, sprinkle with the scallions, drizzle with the sauce, and serve.

Chapter 5: Staples and sauces

Mayonnaise, sriracha sauce, hot chili sauce, and many other frequently used condiments for sushi rolls have been transformed into tasty sauces. These sauces are discussed in this segment, but it also includes common recipes from several sushi restaurants around the world, standard Japanese sauce recipes (such as Ponzu and Miso Sesame sauce), and many recipes that are cited in this text. These sauce recipes are very simple to prepare, flexible for many meals, and some will stay in the fridge for a while. If you are adopting a gluten-free diet, make sure to use gluten-free soy sauce.

5.1 Spicy Mayonnaise Sauce

GLUTEN-FREE, NUT-FREE, VEGETARIAN

Needless to say, this is the most famous spicy sauce in the sushi world. Sriracha is a great sauce on its own, but when you mix it with other condiments, such as mayo, soy sauce, or miso, it can take on a whole new delicious flavor! You can use a spoon to drizzle sushi rolls with this sauce, but using a dressing bottle is better for creating impressive final presentations.

Yield: about ⅓ cup

Prep time: 5 minutes

Cook time: 3 minutes

Ingredients:

- ¼ cup mayonnaise
- 1 tablespoon sriracha sauce
- 1 teaspoon toasted sesame oil

Directions:

In a small bowl, mix the mayonnaise, sriracha sauce, and sesame oil.

5.2 Ginger Dressing

GLUTEN-FREE, NUT-FREE, VEGAN

This dressing is one of my favorite nontraditional Japanese recipes. When I had this at an Asian restaurant in Philadelphia for the first time, I asked the staff for the recipe because it was amazingly delicious! A food processor does all the work for you after you prepare the ingredients. To store, transfer the dressing to a glass jar and keep in the refrigerator for up to 2 weeks.

Yield: 1½ Cup

Prep time: 10 minutes

Cook time: 5 minutes

Ingredients:

- 1 large carrot, coarsely chopped
- ½ large onion, coarsely chopped
- 1 (3- to 4-inch) piece fresh ginger, peeled and coarsely chopped
- 1 garlic clove
- ¼ cup soy sauce (gluten-free if necessary)

- ¼ cup of rice vinegar
- ½ teaspoon salt
- 1 tablespoon toasted sesame oil ½ cup extra-virgin olive oil

Directions:

In a food processor, combine the carrot, onion, ginger, garlic, soy sauce, rice vinegar, salt, sesame oil, and olive oil. Blend until somewhat smooth.

Transfer to a jar, cover, and keep refrigerated. Use within 2 weeks.

COOKING TIP: On the first day, the vegetables and the oil may seem barely mixed, but the dressing reaches the right consistency after a few days.

5.3 Japanese Egg Omelet

GLUTEN-FREE, NUT-FREE, VEGETARIAN

A Japanese egg omelet is basically a thick, soft, fried egg. This savory egg omelet is an original recipe I grew up with. Some other Japanese egg omelet recipes include sugar to add a slightly sweet taste. I will introduce you to two ways of making this dish. The real keys to a successful omelet are to use a nonstick pan and nonstick spray and to preheat the pan really well.

Yield: 1 omelet or 10 pieces for nigiri or 4 sticks for sushi rolls

Prep time: 5 minutes

Cook time: 5 minutes

Ingredients:

- 3 large eggs, beaten
- 2 teaspoons soy sauce (gluten-free if necessary)
- Nonstick cooking spray

TO MAKE THE TRADITIONAL VERSION

1. In a mixing bowl, stir together the eggs and soy sauce.

2. Coat a preheated nonstick rectangular skillet (5 to 6 inches by 7 inches) with cooking spray and pour one-third of the egg mixture into the skillet, being sure to spread the egg over the entire surface of the pan. Cook over medium heat for 20 seconds until the edge of the egg is cooked and liquid is still present on top.

3. Fold the egg in three. It is okay if the egg is unshaped at this moment. Slide the egg to the far side of the pan.

4. Pour half of the remaining mixture into the empty space of the pan, lift the existing egg omelet, and let the mixture flow underneath while spreading the egg all over the surface of the pan. Cook for 30 seconds and fold into three again, then slide the egg to the far side of the pan. Repeat with the remaining egg mixture. Gently press the omelet with the spatula, and cook for 30 seconds on each side.

TO MAKE AN EASIER VERSION

1. In a mixing bowl, stir together the eggs and soy sauce.

2. Coat a preheated 8-inch nonstick skillet with cooking spray and pour all of the egg mixtures into the skillet. Cook over medium-low heat for 1 minute, without stirring, and until the edges of the eggs are slightly cooked.

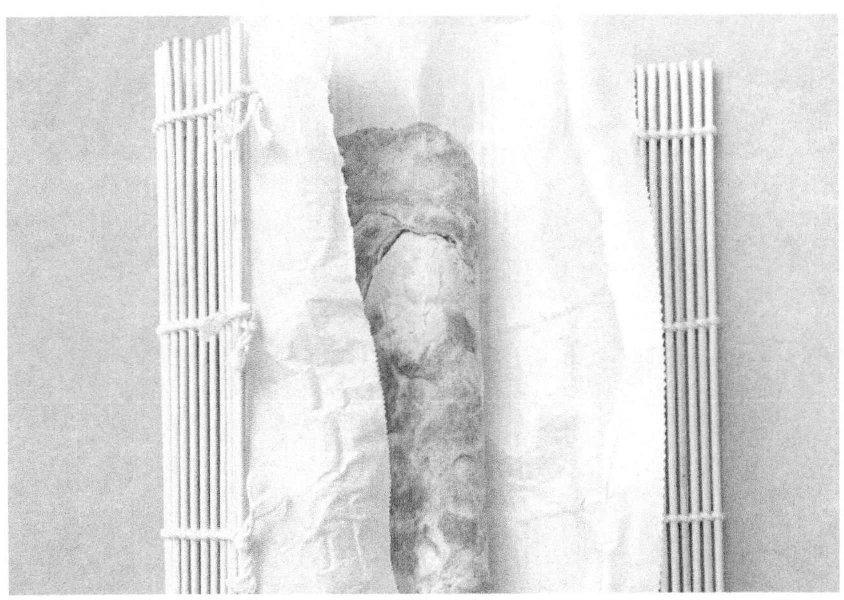

Using a spatula, gently gather the cooked part toward the center of the skillet and spread the uncooked egg toward the edges of the pan. Cook for 1 minute until the egg is set.

Fold the egg in three, gently press the omelet with the spatula, and cook for 30 seconds on each side.

Place the makisu on a work surface and cover with a piece of parchment paper or paper towel. Lay the omelet on it and wrap it with the makisu to make a 1-inch-thick rectangle. Let it sit for 10 minutes at room temperature.

COOKING TIP: The omelet, wrapped in the makisu, can be stored in the refrigerator for about 2 hours to cool, so the omelet acquires a firmer shape.

5.4 Tempura Batter

GLUTEN-FREE, NUT-FREE, VEGAN

I always try to make tempura with a great crunchy (not greasy) texture because it is more delicious that way. The tempura batter recipe has a major effect on the crunchiness. Sometimes tempura batter contains egg, but I use rice vinegar instead, and it works great! The key is to use really cold water (you can even add a few ice cubes to the water before you mix) and not to overmix. That is all you need to cook delicious, crispy tempura.

Yield: 1 cup

Prep time: 10 minutes

Cook time: 5 minutes

Ingredients:

½ cup cornstarch

- 1 teaspoon rice vinegar
- 1 teaspoon salt
- ½ cup of cold water

Directions:

In a small bowl, stir together the cornstarch, rice vinegar, salt, and cold water, and stir very gently until just a few lumps are left.

5.5 Ponzu Sauce

GLUTEN-FREE, NUT-FREE, VEGAN

Ponzu is an essential sauce in Japan and is used almost as much as soy sauce. It contains vinegar and lime juice, so it has a fresher taste than soy sauce. Japanese people use this sauce for many dishes, such as shabu-shabu, grilled fish, dim sum, fried rice, and tofu.

Yield: ½ cup

Prep time: 5 minutes

Cook time: 3 minutes

Ingredients:

- ¼ cup soy sauce (gluten-free if necessary)
- ¼ cup of rice vinegar
- Juice of ½ lime

Directions:

1. Combine the soy sauce, rice vinegar, and lime juice in a jar and keep in the refrigerator for up to 2 weeks.

5.6 Sweet Eel Sauce

GLUTEN-FREE, NUT-FREE, VEGAN

This sauce has a perfect sweet-savory taste and a thick texture. Because the sauce needs to be cooked to get the right consistency, you might want to make this sauce first in your cooking process. Or you can make this sauce ahead of time, keep it in the refrigerator, and use it within 1 month. If the sauce becomes very thick in the refrigerator, keep it at room temperature for at least 1 hour before you use it.

Yield: ½ cup

Prep time: 10 minutes

Cook time: 25 minutes

Ingredients:

- ½ cup soy sauce (gluten-free if necessary)
- ½ cup mirin
- ¼ cup cooking sake
- 2 tablespoons sugar

Directions:

1. In a saucepan, stir together the soy sauce, mirin, cooking sake, and sugar. Bring it to a boil over medium heat. Reduce the heat to low, simmer for 20 minutes, and occasionally stir until thickened. Let it cool for 10 minutes at room temperature.
2. Place the mixture in a sterilized 4-ounce dressing bottle and store it in the refrigerator for up to 1 month.

5.7 Spicy Mango Sauce

GLUTEN-FREE, NUT-FREE, VEGETARIAN

This mango sauce has a very fruity and slightly spicy taste. Unlike tomato salsa, the main ingredients are mango and cilantro, so the texture is very soft. It goes really well with seafood and salads! Mango has a pit in the center like an avocado, but it is very small and sticks to the meat firmly. To remove, cut along the pit, and peel and dice with extra care because it is slippery.

Yield: 1 cup

Prep time: 10 minutes

Cook time: 5 minutes

Ingredients:

- 1 large mango, peeled and diced
- 5 cilantro sprigs, trimmed and finely minced
- ½ teaspoon salt
- Pinch freshly ground black pepper
- 2 teaspoons crushed red pepper
- 2 teaspoons rice vinegar

- Teaspoon grated garlic
- Teaspoons honey
- 2 teaspoons freshly squeezed lemon juice

Directions:

1. In a mixing bowl, stir together the mango, cilantro, salt, black pepper, red pepper, vinegar, garlic, honey, and lemon juice.

2. Transfer to an 8-ounce jar, cover, and keep in the refrigerator for up to 1 week.

5.8 Pico de Gallo

GLUTEN-FREE, NUT-FREE, VEGAN

I was so happy when I learned this recipe. I love fresh tomatoes, but I didn't know many fresh tomato sauce recipes. This Pico de Gallo is easy, is versatile, and lasts for a week in the refrigerator. Increase or decrease jalapeño and garlic according to your preference. You might also consider using lemon instead of lime, but lime has a less sour taste than lemon and adds a touch of that special lime flavor to the dish.

Yield: 2 cups

Prep time: 10 minutes

Cook time: 5 minutes

Ingredients:

- 2 large tomatoes, seeded and diced
- 10 cilantro sprigs, trimmed and minced
- ½ red onion, diced
- 2 teaspoons grated garlic
- ½ teaspoon salt

- ½ jalapeño, seeded and finely diced
- Juice of 1 lime

Directions:

1. In a mixing bowl, stir together the tomatoes, cilantro, onion, garlic, salt, jalapeño, and lime juice.
2. Transfer to a 16-ounce jar, cover, and keep in the refrigerator for up to 1 week.

5.9 Tempura Dashi Sauce

GLUTEN-FREE, NUT-FREE, VEGAN

This is a light-textured, soy sauce-based sauce that has a delicious dashi flavor. Traditionally, tempura is served with this sauce or sea salt. People tend to add grated daikon radish to the sauce; the daikon works as a palate freshener for fried food. The sauce is also used as a condiment for many dishes and is a great base for soup.

Yield: 1 cup

Prep time: 5 minutes

Cook time: 5 minutes

Ingredients:

- 1 cup of water
- 1 teaspoon Shimaya kombu dashi soup stock powder, or any vegetable - or fish -based dashi powder
- ¼ cup soy sauce (gluten-free if necessary)
- ¼ cup mirin

Directions:

1. In a saucepan, stir together the water, dashi powder, soy sauce, and mirin. Bring to a boil over medium heat. Let it cool down.
2. Transfer to an 8-ounce jar, cover, and keep in the refrigerator for up to 1 month.

5.10 Wasabi Mayonnaise Sauce

GLUTEN-FREE, NUT-FREE, VEGETARIAN

There is store-bought wasabi mayonnaise, but this recipe is easy, quick, and customizable to your taste! In this recipe, a dash of soy sauce adds a slightly salty, delicious flavor. This Japanese-style spicy mayonnaise is great for salad, grilled meat, grilled fish, and a fried egg. Also, if you like yakisoba, Japanese stir-fried noodles, try adding this sauce. It is delicious!

Yield: ¼ cup

Prep time: 5 minutes

Cook time: 5 minutes

Ingredients:

- ¼ cup mayonnaise
- 2 teaspoons wasabi
- 1 teaspoon soy sauce (gluten-free if necessary)

In a small bowl, stir together the mayonnaise, wasabi, and soy sauce.

5.11 Soy Sauce Mayonnaise Sauce

GLUTEN-FREE, NUT-FREE, VEGETARIAN

This is a traditional Japanese seasoning mixture that I used earlier in my life to mask the taste of fish and vegetables, which I didn't like very much. This sauce is also a great marinade for fish, meat, and tofu. Sometimes mayonnaise sauces are mixed ahead of time and are transferred into jars or dressing bottles for storage. My preference, however, is to use them fresh, in order to avoid changes in texture and taste.

Yield: 1/3 cup

Prep time: 5 minutes

Cook time: 5 minutes

Ingredients:

- ¼ cup mayonnaise
- 2 tablespoons soy sauce (gluten-free if necessary)

In a small bowl, stir together the mayonnaise and soy sauce.

5.12 Sweet-and-Sour Sauce

GLUTEN-FREE, NUT-FREE, VEGAN

It may surprise you how easily you can make this delicious sauce! You can store this sauce in your refrigerator for up to 2 weeks. It's great to have on hand because it is amazing with sautéed vegetables, grilled meat, or fish. You should always use clean cutlery when serving a sauce, and it is also important to check the look and smell of any sauce before consuming it.

Yield: ¼ cup

Prep time: 5 minutes

Cook time: 5 minutes

Ingredients:

- 2 tablespoons sweet chili sauce
- 1 tablespoon ketchup
- 1 tablespoon soy sauce (gluten-free if necessary)

Directions:

1. Combine the chili sauce, ketchup, and soy sauce.
2. Transfer to a 4-ounce jar and keep in the refrigerator for up to 2 weeks.

5.13 Miso Sesame Sauce

GLUTEN-FREE, NUT-FREE, VEGAN

This is a slightly sweet and highly nutritious sauce. Traditionally, this sauce is used with fried cutlets in Japan, but it's also great with raw vegetables, cold tofu, and Japanese udon noodles. You can use any type of miso and sesame seeds. You can find red miso paste, white miso paste, and mixed (awase) miso in many Asian markets. Red miso paste is salty, white miso is sweet, and awase is a balance of salty and sweet.

Yield: 1/3 cup

Prep time: 5 minutes

Cook time: 5 minutes

Ingredients:

- 2 tablespoons roasted sesame seeds
- 2 tablespoons miso paste
- 2 teaspoons toasted sesame oil
- 1 tablespoon sugar
- 2 teaspoons water

Directions:

1. In a mixing bowl, stir together the sesame seeds, miso, sesame oil, and sugar. Whisk in the water until you have a consistency you like.
2. Transfer to a 4-ounce jar and keep in the refrigerator for up to 3 weeks.

5.14 Sweet Chili Mayonnaise Sauce

GLUTEN-FREE, NUT-FREE, VEGETARIAN

This sauce has a delicious Thai flavor and an amazing combination of sweet, spicy, and sour tastes. In Japan, the sauce is commonly used for cooked shrimp dishes. Also, it is great for grilled chicken, summer rolls, and sandwiches, and as a dipping sauce for vegetables. This chili sauce has a milder taste than the Spicy Mayonnaise Sauce.

Yield: ¼ cup

Prep time: 5 minutes

Cook time: 5 minutes

Ingredients:

- ¼ cup mayonnaise
- 1 tablespoon sweet chili sauce

In a small bowl, stir together the mayonnaise and the chili sauce.

5.15 Peanut Sauce

GLUTEN-FREE, VEGAN

The Asian flavors of cumin, sesame oil, ginger, and garlic make this peanut sauce amazingly delicious and complementary to sushi rolls! Peanuts have a high antioxidant effect, can help with fatigue, and are full of niacin, which means they help prevent hangovers. Make sure to use no-sugar-added and no-salt-added peanut butter because it is healthier, and it is easy to adjust the taste to your preference.

Yield: 1/3 cups

Prep time: 5 minutes

Cook time: 5 minutes

Ingredients:

- 2 tablespoons no-sugar-added and no-salt-added peanut butter
- 1 tablespoon soy sauce (gluten-free if necessary)
- 1 teaspoon cumin
- 1 teaspoon peeled, grated fresh ginger

- 1 teaspoon grated garlic
- 1 teaspoon toasted sesame oil
- 1 teaspoon onion powder
- Juice of ½ lemon
- Salt
- Freshly ground black pepper
- 3 tablespoons warm water, as needed

Directions:

1. In a mixing bowl, stir together the peanut butter, soy sauce, cumin, ginger, garlic, sesame oil, onion powder, and lemon juice. Taste and season with salt and black pepper as needed. Whisk in the warm water until you have a consistency you like.
2. Transfer to a 4-ounce container and keep in the refrigerator for up to 2 weeks.

5.16 Pickling Liquid

GLUTEN-FREE, NUT-FREE, VEGAN

This is a refreshing, ginger-flavored pickling liquid. This is great not only for pickling vegetables but also as a dressing and a sauce for many dishes. I love adding some pickling liquid to a rice cooker when I cook rice. Make a batch of the pickling liquid ahead of time, keep it refrigerated, and use within 3 weeks. Having this liquid in your refrigerator makes your cooking process much easier!

Yield: 1 cup

Prep time: 5 minutes

Cook time: 3 minutes

Ingredients:

- ½ cup toasted sesame oil
- ¼ cup soy sauce (gluten-free if necessary)
- ¼ cup of rice vinegar
- ½ teaspoon salt
- 1 teaspoon peeled, grated fresh ginger

Directions:

1. Combine the sesame oil, soy sauce, rice vinegar, salt, and ginger in an 8-ounce jar. Cover and shake to combine.
2. Store in the refrigerator for up to 3 weeks.

5.17 Almond Sauce

GLUTEN-FREE, VEGAN

This sauce has a simple, light taste, so you can use it with any kind of dishes, such as salad, pasta, and sautéed dishes. Almonds are richer in nutrients and have a higher amount of vitamin E than other nuts. They are also high in minerals and fiber. This sauce can be stored for 2 weeks in the refrigerator, but be sure to stir well every time before you use the sauce.

Yield: ¼ cup

Prep time: 5 minutes

Cook time: 3 minutes

Ingredients:

- 2 tablespoon no-sugar-added and no-salt-added almond butter
- Juice of ½ lemon
- ¼ teaspoon salt
- ½ tablespoon Freshly ground black pepper
- ¼ teaspoon onion powder

- ½ teaspoon grated garlic
- 3 tablespoons warm water, as needed

Directions:

1. In a mixing bowl, stir together the almond butter, lemon juice, salt, pepper, onion powder, and garlic. Whisk in the warm water until you have a consistency you like.
2. Transfer to a 4-ounce jar and keep in the refrigerator for up to 2 weeks.

5.18 Pickled Sushi Ginger (Gari)

GLUTEN-FREE, NUT-FREE, VEGAN

Sushi ginger recipes call for young ginger, which is also called spring ginger. Young ginger tastes mild (you can even eat it raw) and has a juicy, soft, smooth texture with a pink blush. If you use regular ginger, not young ginger, slice very thinly and soak in water for at least 12 to 24 hours before starting to prepare this recipe. Even if the ginger is prepared properly, the taste may still be spicy, and the texture may still be tough and fibrous.

Yield: 1/3 cup

Prep time: 10 minutes, plus 12 hours to marinate

Cook time: 2 minutes

Ingredients:

- 3 ounces young ginger
- ½ cup of rice vinegar
- 1 tablespoon sugar
- 1 teaspoon salt

Directions:

1. Peel the ginger with a small spoon if it has thick skin. Slice very thinly with a slicer or peeler.
2. Fill a saucepan with water. Bring the water to a boil over high heat, add the ginger, and cook for 2 minutes. Drain and let it cool.
3. Combine the vinegar, sugar, and salt and microwave for 20 seconds to melt the sugar. Mix well.
4. Wring out the ginger by hand and add the ginger and the sauce to a 4-ounce jar. Marinate in the refrigerator for at least 12 hours.

5.19 Tempura Batter Bits (Agedama or Tenkasu)

GLUTEN-FREE, NUT-FREE, VEGAN

Tempura batter bits are often used as a garnish for side dishes because the bits actually have a hearty flavor from the tempura ingredients. The best tips to cook great agedama are to use a nonstick skillet and to move a small spoon in a circular motion over the skillet when you drop the batter in, so the small drops of the batter are splashed evenly in the oil.

Yield: ¼ cup

Prep time: 5 minutes

Cook time: 15 minutes

Ingredients:

- 2 tablespoons cornstarch
- 2 tablespoons water
- ½ teaspoon salt
- Vegetable oil, for frying

Directions:

1. In a small bowl, stir together the cornstarch, water, and salt.
2. In a nonstick skillet, heat ½ inch of vegetable oil over medium-low heat until it shimmers. Using a small spoon, put small drops of the mixture in the oil until the dots of the mixture almost cover the bottom of the pan. Fry for 4 to 5 minutes, occasionally stirring, until it browns slightly. Using a mesh skimmer, transfer the bits to a plate lined with paper towels to drain. Repeat with the remaining mixture.
3. When it cools down, transfer to a freezer bag and store in the freezer for up to 1 month. Use without thawing.

5.20 Planning Your Sushi Feast

The best for entertaining is hand-rolled (temaki) sushi at a sushi gathering. It is quick to plan for the hosts, and visitors will enjoy sushi "build-your-own."

How to Cook Temaki Sushi for a Party

- ✓ Cook 1 cup of rice with sushi per user. Put the rice with a rice paddle in a wide bowl and cover it with a damp kitchen towel and hold it ready for use at room temperature.
- ✓ Get the vegetables and fried fillings packed.
- ✓ Line some broken lettuce leaves with a serving plate and place each filling on a slice of lettuce.
- ✓ Along with the serving tray, supply chopsticks or small tongs.
- ✓ Cooked food may be prepared ahead of time and frozen for up to 1 month, such as fried chicken and shrimp tempura. You should reheat for 10 to 20 minutes, depending on the amount, in a 400 ° F oven on the day of the gathering.

- ✓ About three times the amount of parts of each ingredient is easier to plan than the number of persons attending.
- ✓ Prepare the fillings for refrigeration.
- ✓ Using different dishes for fish and shellfish is preferred.
- ✓ Hold it refrigerated before ready to eat.
- ✓ Prepare between two or three times the amount of parts of each ingredient as the number of individuals participating.

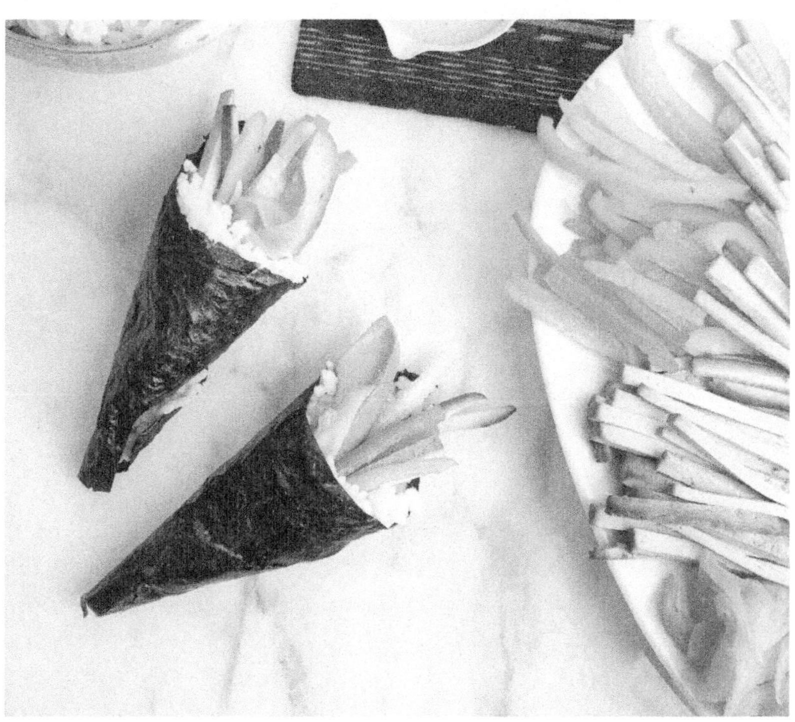

5.21 Prepare Wraps

Serve on a plate with nori, spinach, and thin fried egg as wrappers.

Directions:

1. Use a whole nori sheet per individual and split it into quarters so that each nori piece is around the square in form.
2. Wash and dry the leaves of the lettuce and tear them to around the same size as the nori split.
3. Cook the thin fried eggs using one egg per visitor (see steps 1 and 2 of Egg and Salmon Roe Temari).
4. Prepare Sauces: For each homemade sauce, use a dressing or squeeze bottles, such as Sweet Eel Sauce, Spicy Mayonnaise Sauce, and/or Miso Sesame Sauce. Getting plain mayonnaise, too, is nice.

Conclusion

Thank you so much for reading it to the end of this book. Most people who appreciate the taste of this distinctive part of Asian food are now learning to cook it at home. In order to produce sushi at home, you don't have to be a top-class cook. All you have to do is boil some rice, dice some fish and veggies, grab some nori, and wrap them all together. The first few attempts might not end up as successful as you planned. Maybe poorly packed rice, perhaps irregular rolls, and some ingredients can fall out. It all takes is a little practice, and you would be able to achieve the perfect sushi form at home.

Printed in Great Britain
by Amazon

71648658R00132